Straight to the Point—ASP.Net 2.0

Straight to the Point

ASP.Net 2.0

DINESH MAIDASANI

B.A., Dip. Comp. Sc.

FIREWALL MEDIA

(An Imprint of Laxmi Publications Pvt. Ltd.)

BANGALORE • CHENNAI • COCHIN • GUWAHATI • HYDERABAD
JALANDHAR • KOLKATA • LUCKNOW • MUMBAI • RANCHI
NEW DELHI • BOSTON, USA

Published by :

FIREWALL MEDIA

(An Imprint of Laxmi Publications Pvt. Ltd.)

113, Golden House, Daryaganj,

New Delhi-110002

Phone : 011-43 53 25 00

Fax : 011-43 53 25 28

www.laxmipublications.com

info@laxmipublications.com

Price : **Rs. 95.00** *Only.* *First Edition* : 2007

OFFICES

India

✆ **Bangalore**	080-26 61 15 61
✆ **Chennai**	044-24 34 47 26
✆ **Cochin**	0484-239 70 04
✆ **Guwahati**	0361-254 36 69, 251 38 81
✆ **Hyderabad**	040-24 65 23 33
✆ **Jalandhar**	0181-222 12 72
✆ **Kolkata**	033-22 27 37 73, 22 27 52 47
✆ **Lucknow**	0522-220 95 78
✆ **Mumbai**	022-24 91 54 15, 24 92 78 69
✆ **Ranchi**	0651-230 77 64

USA

Boston

11, Leavitt Street, Hingham,

MA 02043, USA

FST-2920-095-STTP_ASP.NET 2.0 **C—14003/07/04**

Typeset at : Kalyani Computer Services, New Delhi. *Printed at* : PRINT O PACK, Delhi

Contents

1 Introduction to ASP using HTML

INTRODUCTION

HTML stands for Hypertext Markup Language. It is used for creating static pages. HTML has its own use and implementation. HTML tags are also used inside the dynamic Web pages of PHP, ASP.Net etc. So it is essential to understand the basic HTML part.

Since this book is on ASP.Net so I will rapidly brush up your skills in necessary HTML.

The basic structure of HTML Web page is like this:

```
<html>
<head>
<title>

</title>

<script language="VBScript">
</script>

</head>

<body>

<h1>
Heading of Web page
</h1>

<?php

PHP script....

?>
```

```
<%
ASP.Net script….

%>

</body>
</html>
```

<html> tag means now the HTML code is going to be start. HTML is not case-sensitive you can use both upper and lower characters. All will be treated same. After <html> we write<head> tag under which you can mention client-side scripting, title and meta/keywords.

```
<html>
<head>
<title>
This is my first Web page
</title>

<script language="VBScript">
</script>

</head>
<body>

<h1>
This is my first Web page
</h1>

<?php

PHP script….

?>

<%
ASP.Net script….
```

```
%>

</body>
</html>
```

Output of the above HTML would be like this:

In above figure you may notice this that title of the Web page is "This is my first Web page" which you have specified in between <title></title> tags.

Now the most important part here to understand is in a HTML page you can also write both client-side and server-side scripting.

Let me elaborate first client-side scripting.

CLIENT-SIDE SCRIPTING

This scripting is used for client-side validations. For example once user has completed the registration form then you need to check that whether he has entered the name in name field or not so before sending the data to server you check this at client-side which will save time because there is no need to send page for such validation purposes to server. The only thing required is that you must be sure that at client-side browser should have capability to execute scripts. You can write client-side scripts using many scripting languages like VBScript, JavaScript etc. Both are popular. To tell the browser in which scripting language you have written script you can instruct in <script language="VbScript or JavaScript" > tags.

For example:

```
<script language = "VBscript">
...
...
.......
</script>
```

The following code will demonstrate this:

```
<html>
<head>
<title>
Client-side scripting example
</title>

<script language="VBScript">

sub btn_onclick

if trim(document.form1.text1.value) = "" then

msgbox("Text field should not be blank")

else

msgbox ("You have entered:= " & document.form1.text1.value)

end if

end sub

</script>
</head>
<body>

<h1>
```

```
Client-side scripting example
</h1>

<form name="form1">

<input type="text" name="text1">
<br>
<br>
<input type="button" value="click me" name="btn" >

</form>

</body>
</html>
```

You can notice this that I'm validating text value. If text value is blank then we are prompting user that blank values are not allowed. Like this you can validate using client-side scripting. Once you are satisfied from your validation then you can send details to server.

```
Document.form1.submit
```

Output of the above HTML would be like the one shown on the next page.

SERVER-SIDE SCRIPTING

You can use both client-side and server-side scripting on one page. To tell the server that particular script will be executed in server you add runat="server" inside script tag.

For example:

```
<script language="vb" runat="Server">

sub run_proc(sender as object, system as eventargs)

commands....
......
......
end sub

</script>
```

The following code will demonstrate this:

```
<html>
<head>
<title>
Server-side scripting example
</title>

<script language="vb" runat="Server">
sub run_proc(sender as object, system as eventargs)
showtext.innerhtml = "You have entered: " & tt.value
end sub
</script>

</head>
<body>
<h1>
Server-side scripting example
</h1>
```

```
<form runat=server>

<input type=text runat=server id=tt>
<br>
<br>
<input type="button" value="Click me " runat=server
onserverclick="run_proc">
<br>
<br>
<span id=showtext runat="Server" />

</form>

</body>
</html>
```

Output of the above code would be like the one shown on the next page.

START AND END TAGS

In HTML you always give start and end tags. End tags are not compulsory for few tags. For example if you want to bold the text then you can use <b> tag for this purpose. You have to give range that how much text you want to make bold so for this purpose you close the range using end tag </b>. End tag contains </ plus tag>

Center

You can align any text in center using <center> tag of HTML.

For example:

```
<center> some text....  </center>
```

The following code will demonstrate this:

```
<html>
<head>
<title>
Center Tag Example
</title>
</head>

<body>
```

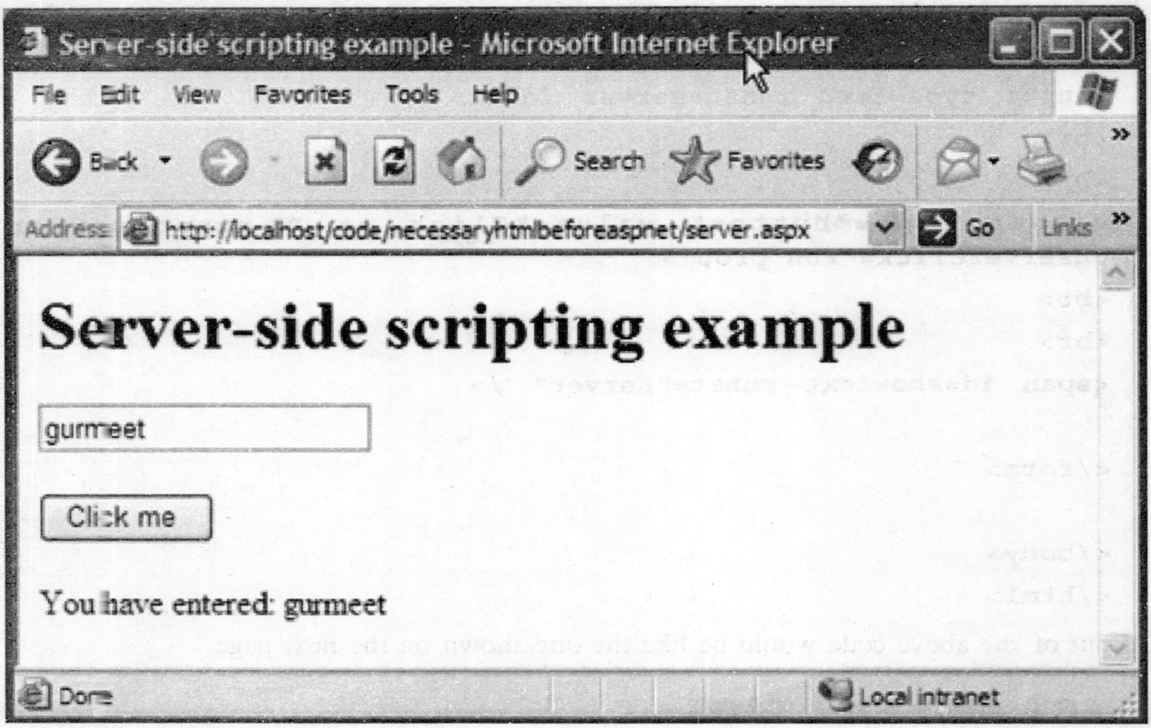


```
<h1>
Center Tag Example
</h1>

<Center> Global Learning with HTML </Center>

</body>
</html>
```

Output of the above HTML would be like the one shown on the next page.

BOLD

You can make any text bold using <b> tag. Once the range has been determined then you have to close the bold tag using </b>. You just need to prefix /.

The following HTML code will demonstrate the use of <b> tag:

```
<html>
<head>
<title>
```

```
Bold Tag Example
</title>
</head>

<body>
<h1>
Bold Tag Example
</h1>

<b> Making text bold </b>

</body>
</html>
```

Output of the above code would be like the one shown on the next page.

ITALIC

You can make any text italic using <i> tag. Once the range has been determined then you have to close the italic tag using </i>. You just need to prefix /.

The following HTML code will demonstrate the use of <i> tag:

```
<html>
```

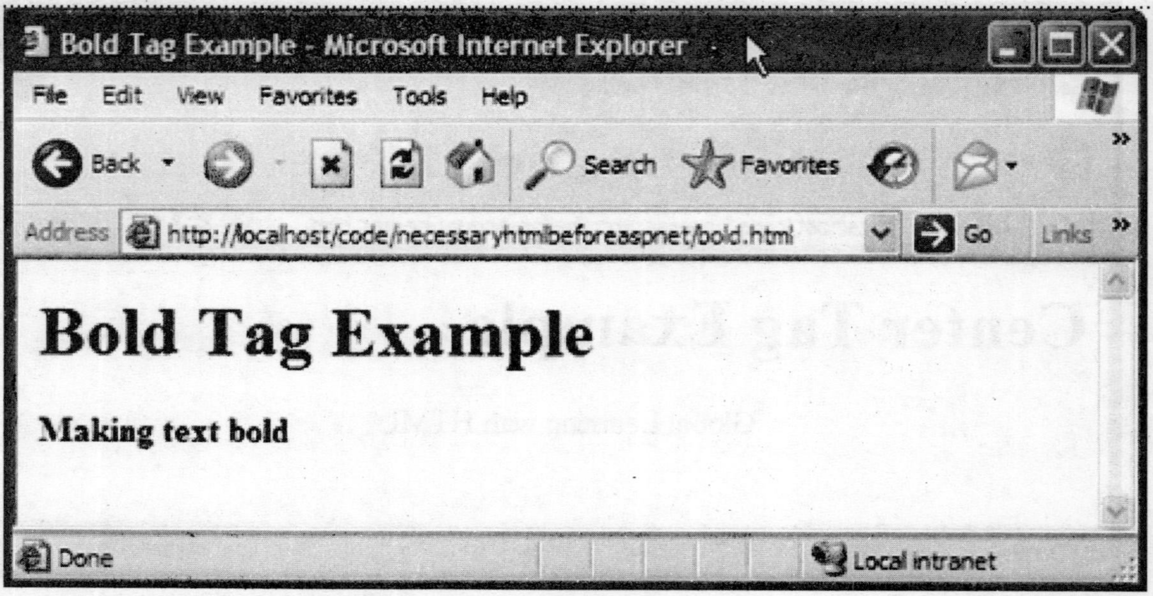


```
<head>
<title>
Italic Tag Example
</title>
</head>

<body>
<h1>
Italic Tag Example
</h1>

<i> Making text Italic </i>

</body>
</html>
```

Output of the above code would be like the one shown on the next page.

UNDERLINE

You can make any text underline using <u> tag. Once the range has been determined then you have to close the underline tag using </u>. You just need to prefix /.

The following HTML code will demonstrate the use of <u> tag:

```
<html>
<head>
<title>
Underline Tag Example
</title>
</head>

<body>
<h1>
Underline Tag Example
</h1>

<u> Making text Underline</u>

</body>
</html>
```

Output of the above code would be like this:

HEADING

You can format any text to highlight it using heading tags like <h1>, <h2>, <h3> etc. Once the range has been determined then you have to close the heading tag using </h1 or 2, 3..>. You just need to prefix /.

The following HTML code will demonstrate the use of <h5> tag:

```
<html>
<head>
<title>
Heading Tag Example
</title>
</head>

<body>
<h1>
Heading Tag Example
</h1>

<h5> Formating text through heading tag h5 </h5>
```

```
</body>
</html>
```

Output of the above code would be like this:

PARAGRAPH

If you want to create paragraphs in your document then you can do this using <p> tag.

The following code will demonstrate the use of <p> tag:

```
<html>
<head>
<title>
Paragraph Tag Example
</title>
</head>

<body>
<h1>
Paragraph Tag Example
</h1>
```

```
<p>
First  Paragraph......
</p>
<p>
Second  Paragraph.....
</p>
<p>
Third  Paragraph......
</p>

</body>
</html>
```

Output of the above code would be like this:

BREAK

If you want to insert breaks between lines in your document then you can perform this using <br> tag.

The following code will demonstrate the use of <br> tag:

```
<html>
<head>
<title>
Break Tag Example
</title>
</head>

<body>
<h1>
Break Tag Example
</h1>

<br>
First Break......
<br>
Second Break.....
<br>
Third Break......

</body>
</html>
```

Output of the above code would be like the one shown on the next page.

FONT

You can change the color, size and style of font using <font> tag. Once the range has been determined regarind font manipulation then you have to close the font tag using </font>. You just need to prefix /.

The following code will demonstrate the use of <font> tag:

```
<html>
<head>
<title>
Font Tag Example
</title>
</head>
```

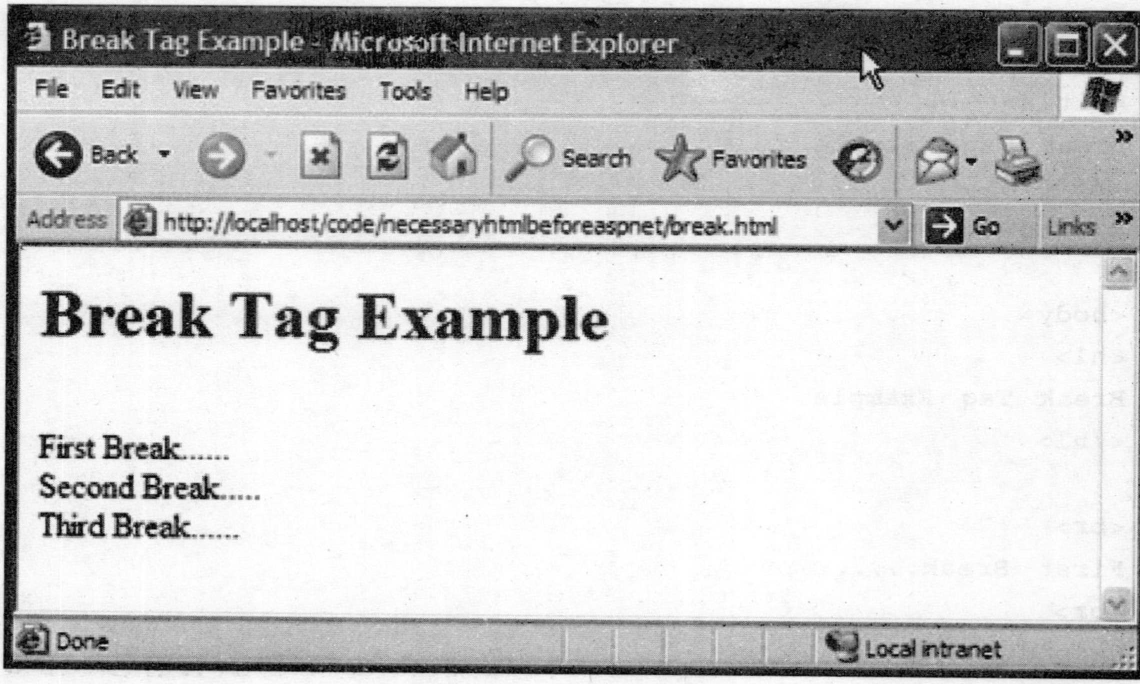


```
<body>
<h1>
Font Tag Example
</h1>

<font face="Arial" size="24" color="red" > Hello World! </font>

</body>
</html>
```

Output of the above code would be like the one shown on the next page.

HORIZONTAL LINE

Using <hr> tag you can add divisions to document. This is a big horizontal line.

The following code will demonstrate the use of <hr> tag:

```
<html>
<head>
<title>
Horizontal Tag Example
```

```
</title>
</head>

<body>
<h1>
Horizontal Tag Example
</h1>

In the valley of creative horizon

<hr>

Singh
<br>
Bill Gates
<br>
Narayan
```

```
</body>
</html>
```

Output of the above code would be like this:

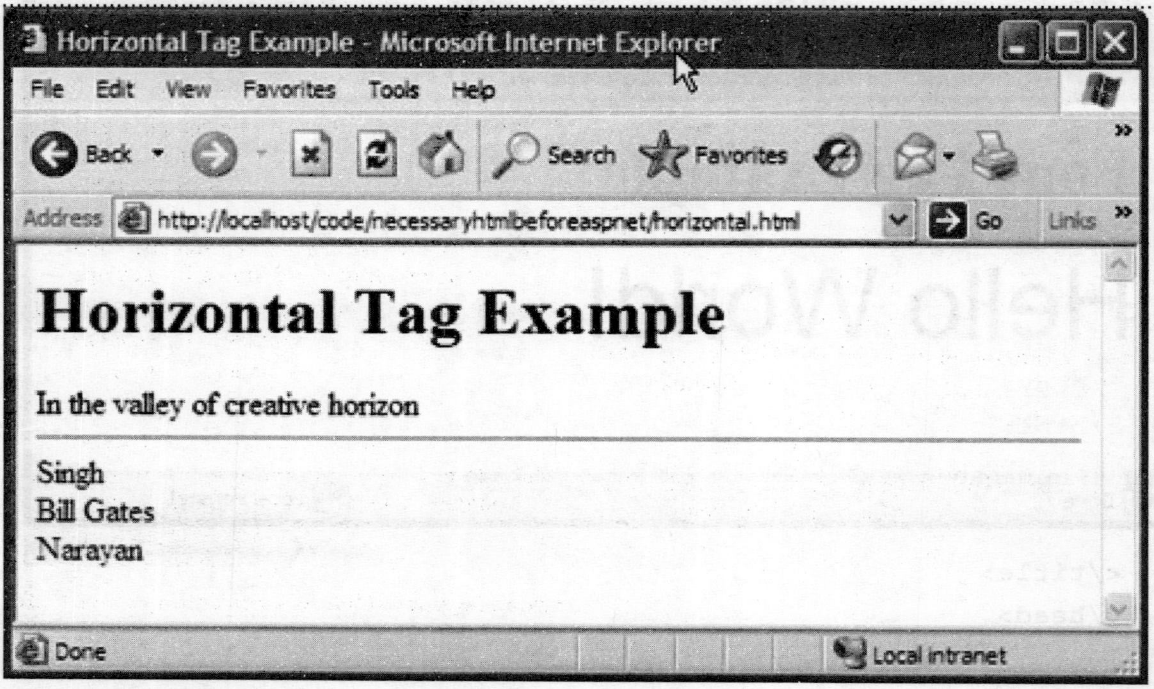

BLOCKQUOTE

To show that particular text is different from the rest of text you can use <blockquote> tag.

The followng code will demonstrate the use of <Blockquote> tag:

```
<html>
<head>
<title>
Blockquote Tag Example
</title>
</head>

<body>
<h1>
Blockquote Tag Example
```

```
</h1>

In the valley of creative horizon

<hr>

Singh
<blockquote>
Bill Gates
</blockquote>
Narayan

</body>
</html>
```

Output of the above code would be like this:

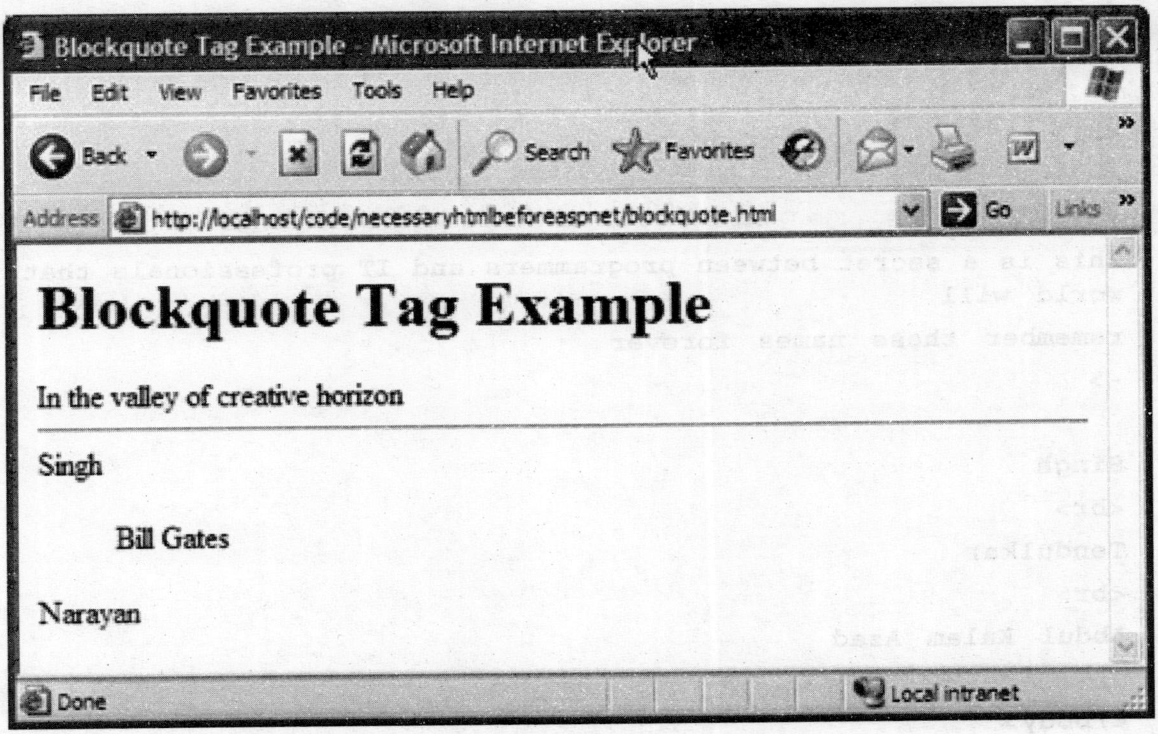

COMMENTS

You can add comments to your HTML document that will be not seen by a visitor. To begin the comment use <! tag and to end the comment use -> tag. The following code will demonstrate the use of comments tag:

```
<html>
<head>
<title>
Blockquote Tag Example
</title>
</head>

<body>
<h1>
Blockquote Tag Example
</h1>

Who are these?

<hr>

<!
This is a secret between programmers and IT professionals that
world will
remember these names forever
->

Singh
<br>
Tendulkar
<br>
Abdul Kalam Azad

</body>
</html>
```

Output of the above HTML would be like the one shown on the next page.

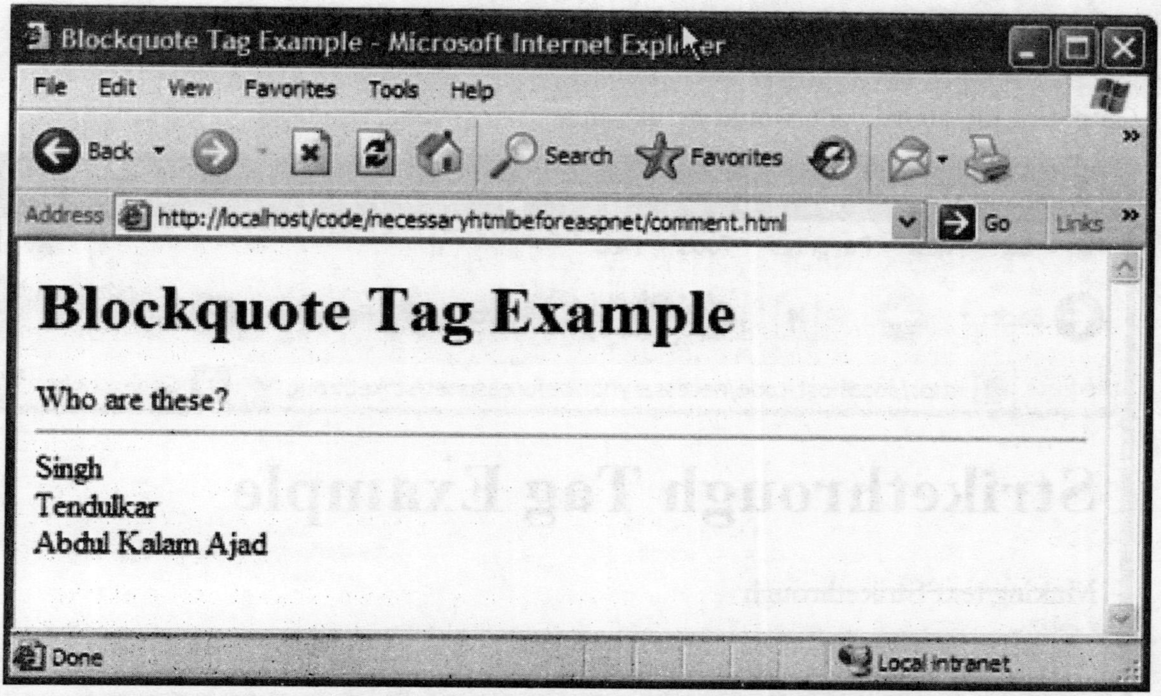

STRIKETHROUGH

This tag draws a horizontal line through the middle of the text using <s> tag. Once the range has been determined then you have to close the strikethrough tag using </s>. You just need to prefix /.

The following code will demonstrate the use of <s> tag:

```
<html>
<head>
<title>
Strikethrough Tag Example
</title>
</head>

<body>
<h1>
Strikethrough Tag Example
</h1>

<s> Making text Strikethrough</s>
```

```
</body>
</html>
```

Output of the above code would be like this:

BIG

<big> tag prints a larger font size to display the text. Once the range has been determined then you have to close the big tag using </big>. You just need to prefix /.

The following code will demonstrate the use of <big> tag:

```
<html>
<head>
<title>
Big Tag Example
</title>
</head>

<body>
<h1>
Big Tag Example
</h1>
```

```
ordinary text
<br>
<br>
<big> Making text big</big>

</body>
</html>
```

Output of the above HTML would be like this:

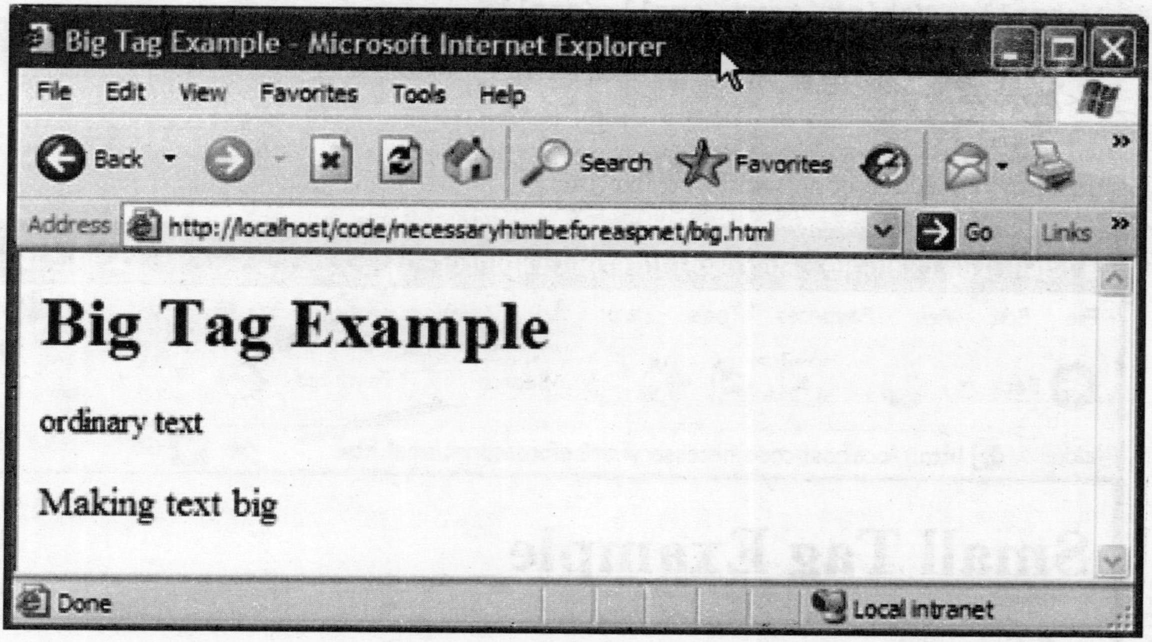

SMALL

<small> tag displays the text in a smaller font size. Once the range has been determined then you have to close the small tag using </small>. You just need to prefix /.

The following code will demonstrate the use of <small> tag:

```
<html>
<head>
<title>
Small Tag Example
</title>
</head>
```

```
<body>
<h1>
Small Tag Example
</h1>

ordinary text
<br>
<br>
<small> Making text small</small>

</body>
</html>
```

Output of the above code would be like this:

SUBSCRIPT

_{tag moves the text lower than the surrounding text. Once the range has been determined then you have to close the subscript tag using}. You just need to prefix /.

The following code will demonstrate the use of <sub> tag:

```
<html>
<head>
<title>
Sub Tag Example
</title>
</head>

<body>
<h1>
Sub Tag Example
</h1>

ordinary text
<br>
<br>
<sub> Making text subscript</sub>

</body>
</html>
```

Output of the above code would be like the one shown on the next page.

SUPERSCRIPT

<sub> tag moves the text higher than the surrounding text. Once the range has been determined then you have to close the superscript tag using </sup>. You just need to prefix /.

The following code will demonstrate the use of <sup> tag:

```
<html>
<head>
<title>
Superscript Tag Example
</title>
</head>

<body>
<h1>
```

```
Superscript Tag Example
</h1>

ordinary text
<br>
<br>
<sup> Making text superscript</sup>

</body>
</html>
```

Output of the above code would be like the one shown on the next page.

LINK

You can create a link using <a> tag. You have to give path of linking file using href attribute. For example:

```
<a href="contactus.html"> Contact Us </a>
```

The following code will demonstrate the use of <a> tag:

```
<html>
<head>
```

```
<title>
<A> Tag Example
</title>
</head>

<body>
<h1>
<A> Tag Example
</h1>

<a href="aboutus.html"> About Us </a>

</body>
</html>
```

Output of the above code would be like the one shown on the next page.

TABLE

You can create table and can placed your data inside it in the form of rows and columns. To create a table you generally use <table> tag. Under <table> tag you specify <tr> and

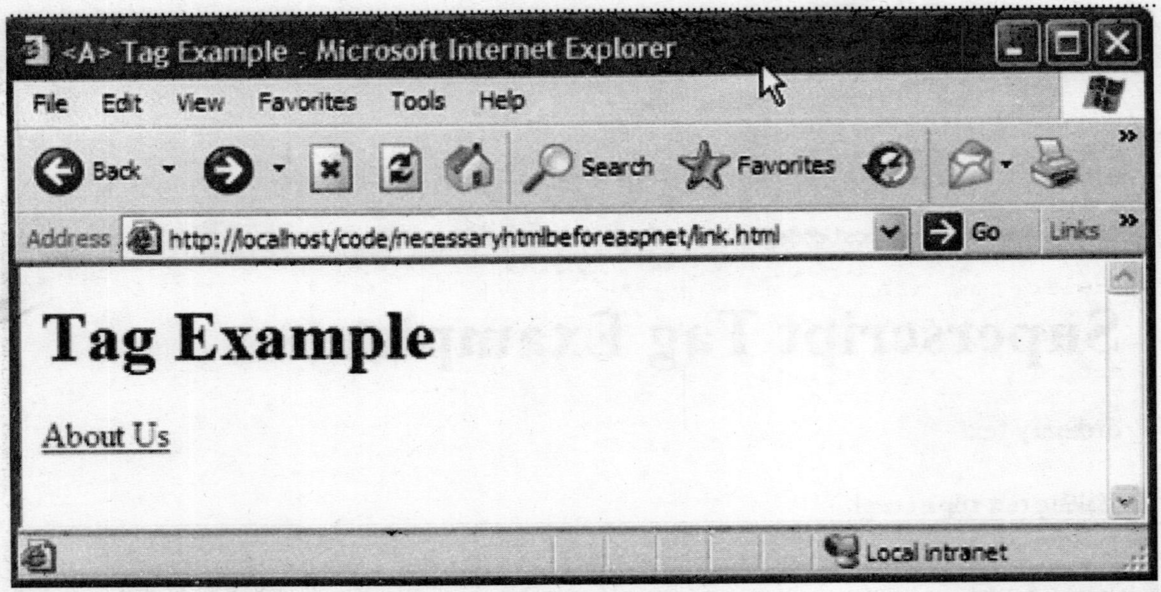

<td> tags which are used for creating rows and columns. You can use them as many rows and columns you want.

For example:

This will create one column and one row

```
<table>
<tr>
<td>
Hello world
</td>
</tr>
</table>
```

This will create three columns and two rows:

```
<table>
<tr>
<td>
Hello world
</td>
<td>
Hello world 2
</td>
```

```
<td>
Hello world 3
</td>
</tr>
<tr>
<td>
Hello world
</td>
<td>
Hello world 2
</td>
<td>
Hello world 3
</td>
</tr>

</table>
```

The following code will demonstrate the implantation:

```
<html>
<head>
<title>
Table Tag Example
</title>
</head>

<body>
<h1>
Table Tag Example
</h1>

<table border=1>
<tr>
<td>
First Row - First column
</td>
```

```
<td>
First Row - Second column 2
</td>
<td>
First Row - Third Column 3
</td>
</tr>

<tr>
<td>
Second Row - First column
</td>
<td>
Second Row - Second column 2
</td>
<td>
Second Row - Third Column 3
</td>
</tr>

<tr>
<td>
Third Row - First column
</td>
<td>
Third Row - Second column 2
</td>
<td>
Third Row - Third Column 3
</td>
</tr>

</table>

</body>
```

```
</html>
```

Output of the above code would be like this:

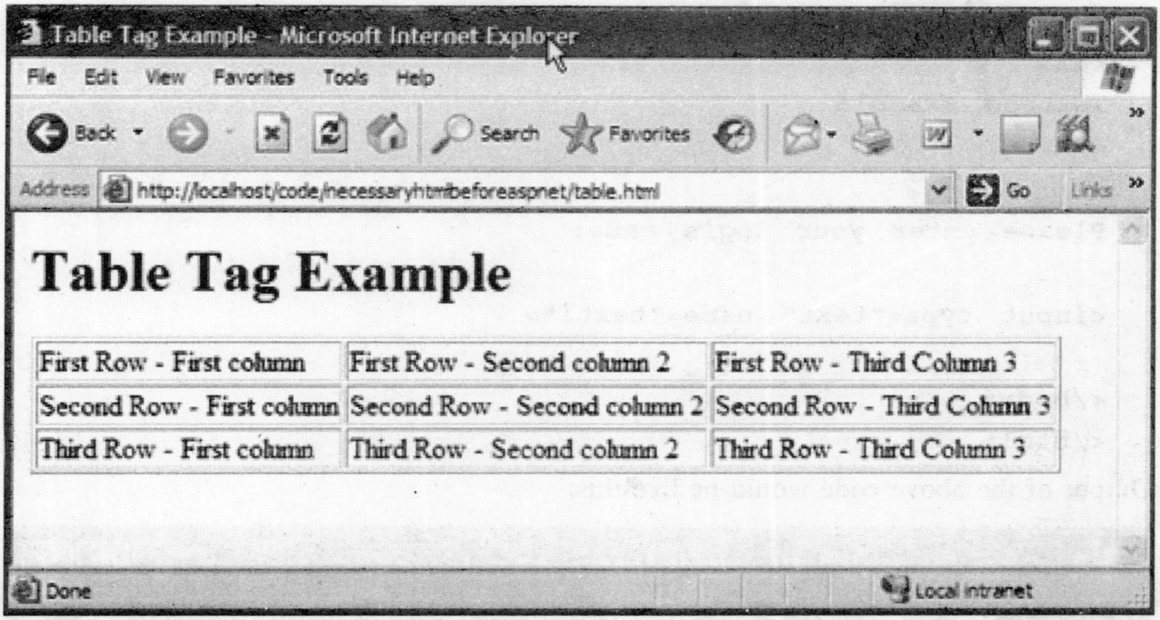

FORM ELEMENT

If you want to accept data from user and send it to server for submission or if you want to validate the data at client-side or server-side then form element plays robust role regarding all these.

You can use <form> and </form> tags and inside it you can use other textbox, radio, checkbox etc elements.

TEXT BOX

The basic purpose of text box is to take information of data from user. For this you have to write following HTML:

```
<input type= text>
```

The following code will demonstrate the use of text box:

```
<html>
<head>
<title>
Textbox Example
</title>
```

```
</head>

<body>
<h1>
Textbox Example
</h1>

Please enter your login name:

<input type="text" name="text1">

</body>
</html>
```

Output of the above code would be like this:

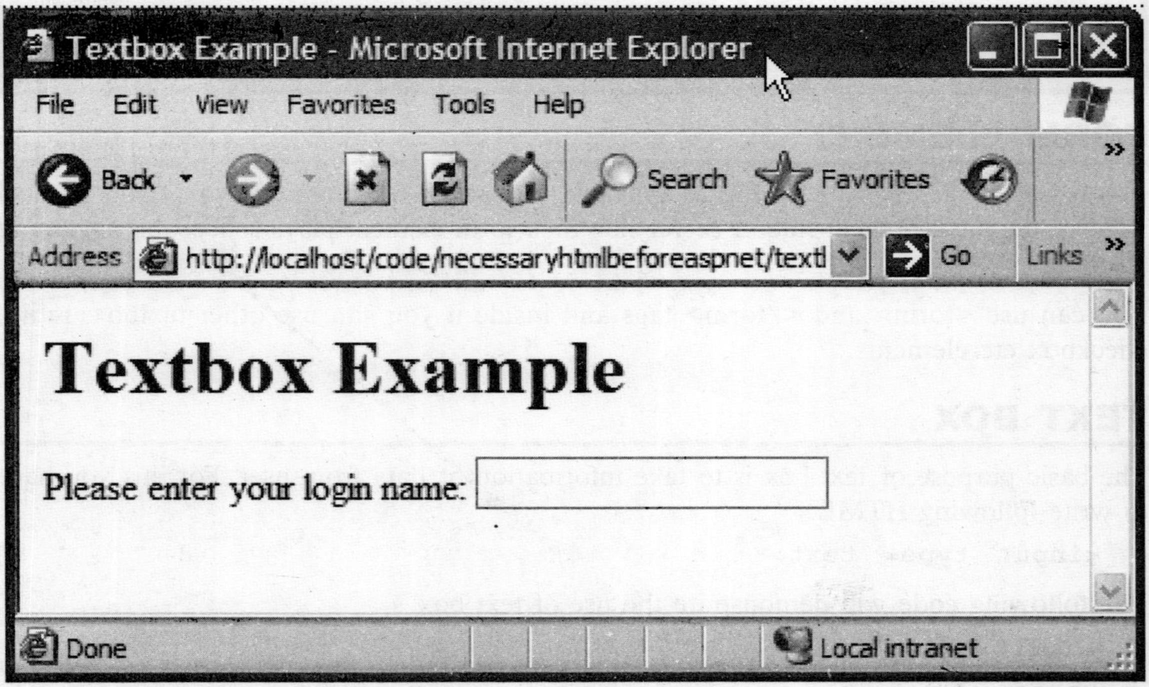

CHECK BOX

Check box is use for selecting multiple values. For this you have to write following HTML:

```
<input type= checkbox >
```

The following code will demonstrate the use of check box:

```
<html>
<head>
<title>
Checkbox Example
</title>
</head>

<body>
<h1>
Checkbox Example
</h1>

Please select your hobbies:

<br>
<br>

<input type="checkbox" name="ch1"> Sports
<input type="checkbox" name="ch2"> Music
<Br>
<br>
<input type="checkbox" name="ch3"> Reading
<input type="checkbox" name="ch4"> Writing

</body>
</html>
```

Output of the above HTML would be like the one shown on the next page.

RADIO BUTTON

Radio button is uses for selecting one value out of multiple values. For this you have to write following HTML:

```
<input type= radio >
```

The following code will demonstrate the use of radio button:

```
<html>
```

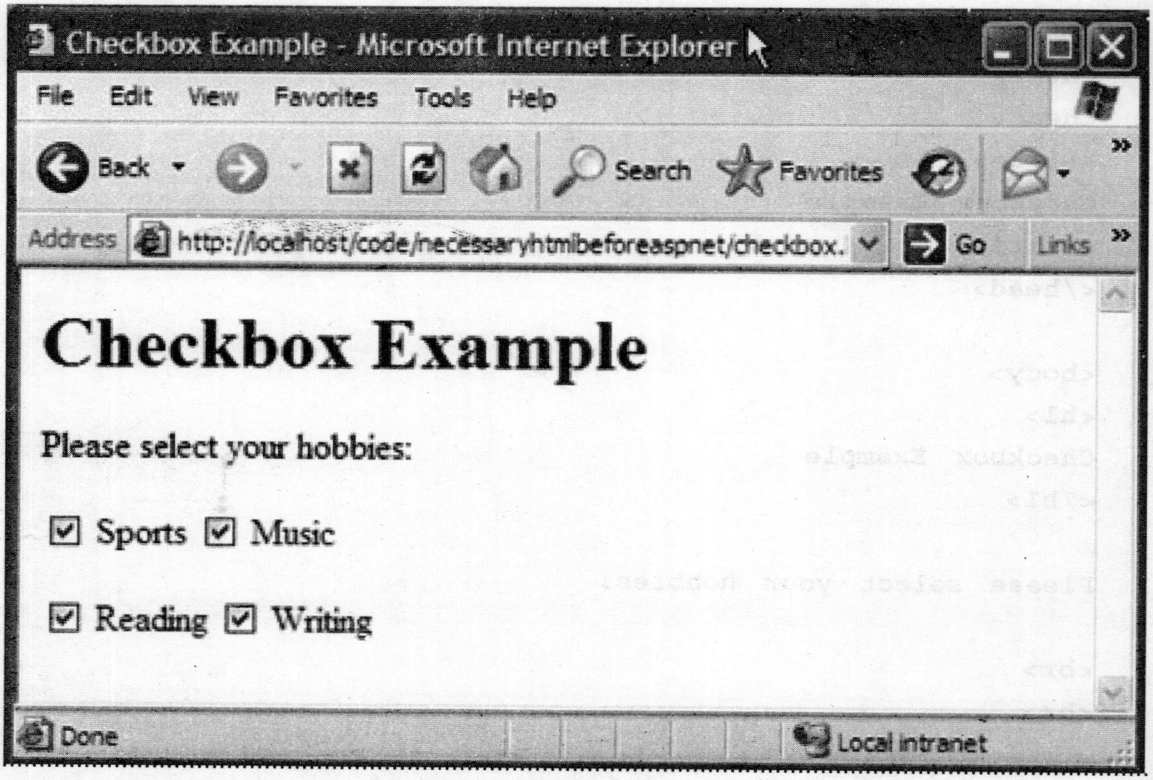


```
<head>
<title>
Radio button Example
</title>
</head>

<body>
<h1>
Radio buttonExample
</h1>

Please select any one hobby:

<br>
<br>
```

```
<input type="radio" name="r1"> Sports
<input type="radio" name="r1"> Music
<Br>
<br>
<input type="radio" name="r1"> Reading
<input type="radio" name="r1"> Writing

</body>
</html>
```

Output of the above code would be like this:

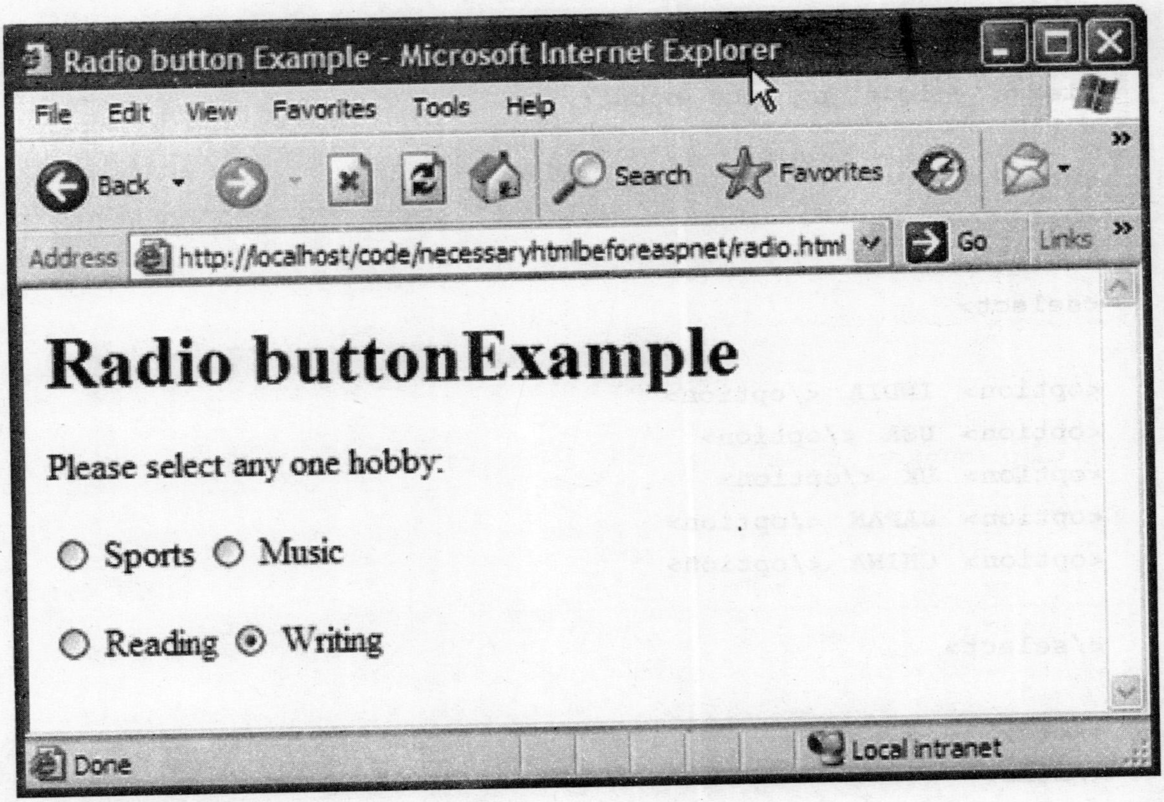

LIST BOX

List box is used to select one value of multiple values. It saves the space because everything contains inside the box and user can select it first clicking on drop-down list.

For example:

The following HTML code will demonstrate the list box:

```
<html>
<head>
<title>
Listbox Example
</title>
</head>

<body>
<h1>
Listbox Example
</h1>

Please select any one country:

<br>
<br>

<select>

<option> INDIA </option>
<option> USA </option>
<option> UK </option>
<option> JAPAN </option>
<option> CHINA </option>

</select>

</body>
</html>
```

Output of the above code would be like the one shown on the next page.

SUBMIT

Submit button plays vital role especially in registration or such forms which accept some data from user. Once submit button is clicked then you can use procedure or function to validate data in a script. If you have not written any script and if submit will find any path

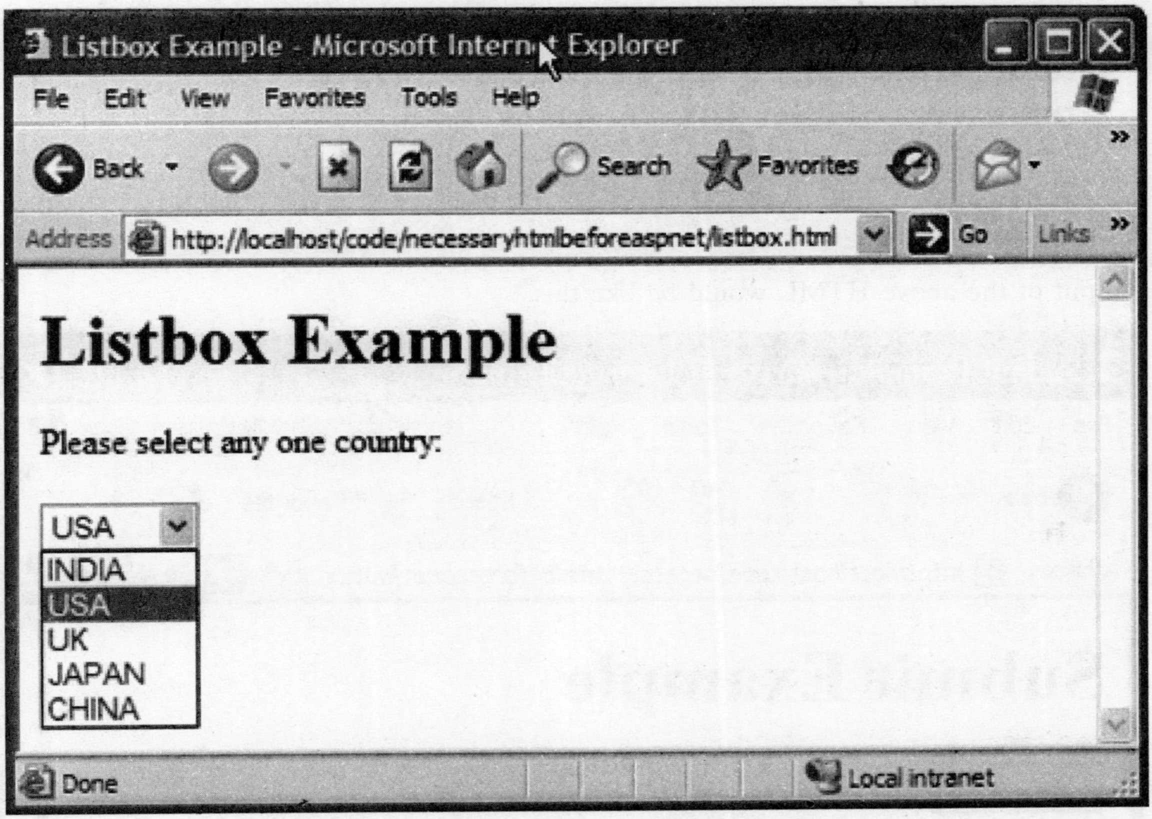

in action attribute of form tag then it will redirect the page to particular location using post or get method. You may also use submit button for any actions or coding which you want to perform in a client-side script for that you can use vbscript or javascript.

You can create button using following code:

```
<input type="submit">
```

The following code will demonstrate submit:

```
<html>
<head>
<title>
Submit Example
</title>
</head>
<body>
<h1>
Submit Example
```

```
</h1>
<form method="post" action="validateform.aspx">
<INPUT TYPE="submit" VALUE="Click me">
</form>
</body>
</html>
```

Output of the above HTML would be like this:

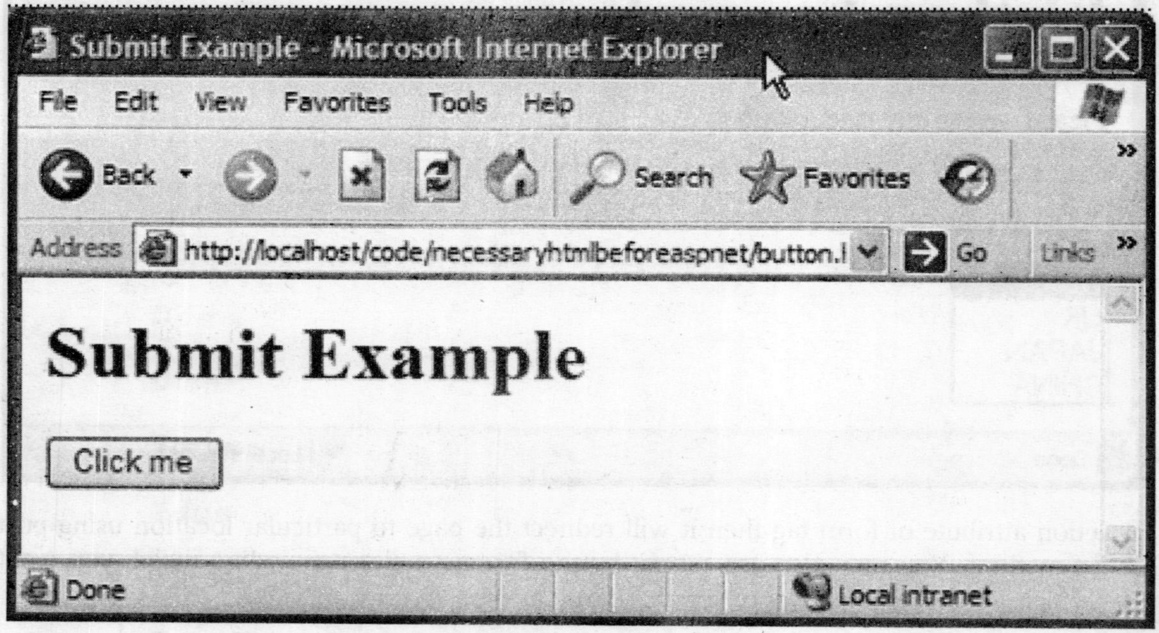

2 Standard Controls of ASP

ADROTATOR CONTROL

The basic purpose of AdRotator control is to show ad images randomly. Whenever visitor clicks on the image it navigates to a new Web page or Web site associated with it.

Every time when user will visit the page the AdRotator control will display different image.

For example:

```
<asp:AdRotator id="ads1" Advertisementfile="Ads.xml"
Borderwidth="1" runat=server />
```

In AdvertisementFile attribute you have to give the name of file which contains the all information related to images like its storage path in Web Server, alternate text which you like to appear and obviously the link details. Whenever visitor will click on the image he/she will be taken to the website which you specify in NavigateUrl attribute. This file is a xml file so you should save it with the .xml extension.

In XML file you can mention the width and height of the image using Width and Height attributes. ImageUrl attribute is compulsory. To make image clickable and to navigate to the Web location you have NavigateUrl attribute. AlternateText attribute behaves just like an ALT tag of HTML. Impression attribute indicates the "weight" of the ad relative to the other ads in the file regarding rotation and Keyword attribute tells the category for the ad for the filteration on page.

The following code will illustrate the use of AdRotator control

— XML File — (adsfile.xml)

```
<Advertisements>
 <Ad>
<Width>300</Width>
<Height>100</Height>
<ImageUrl>banner1.gif</ImageUrl>
<NavigateUrl>http://www.yahoo.com</NavigateUrl>
<AlternateText>Goes to yahoo web site</AlternateText>
<Impressions>40</Impressions>
<keyword> Education </keyword>
```

```
  </Ad>

  <Ad>

 <Width>300</Width>
 <Height>100</Height>
 <ImageUrl>banner2.gif</ImageUrl>
 <NavigateUrl>http://www.google.com</NavigateUrl>
 <AlternateText>Goes to google web site</AlternateText>
 <Impressions>25</Impressions>
 <keyword> Education </keyword>

  </Ad>

  <Ad>

 <Width>300</Width>
 <Height>100</Height>
 <ImageUrl>banner3.gif</ImageUrl>
 <NavigateUrl>http://www.msn.com</NavigateUrl>
 <AlternateText>Goes to msn web site</AlternateText>
 <Impressions>35</Impressions>
 <keyword> Education </keyword>

  </Ad>

 </Advertisements>
```

— Aspx file —

```
 <html>
 <head>
 <title>
 Adrotator Control example
 </title>
 </head>
```

```
<body>
<h1>
Adrotator Control example
</h1>

<form runat=server>

<asp:AdRotator id="ads1" AdvertisementFile="adsfile.xml"
BorderWidth="1" runat=server />

</form>

</body>
</html>
```

Output of the above code would be like the one shown on the next page.

BULLETEDLIST CONTROL

It is used to create a list of items. Every item is formatted with bullet. To display the individual list items you have to place a ListItem object for all entries between opening and closing tags of BulletedList control.

For example:

```
<asp:BulletedList   BulletStyle="circle" runat=server>

   <asp:ListItem>Item</asp:ListItem>

            </asp:BulletedList>
```

BulletedList control is also used to render a list of hyperlinks. For this you have to set the BulletedList.DisplayMode property to BulletedListDisplayMode.HyperLink.

The following code will illustrate the BulletedList control implementation:

```
<html>
<head>
<title>
BulletedList Control Example
```

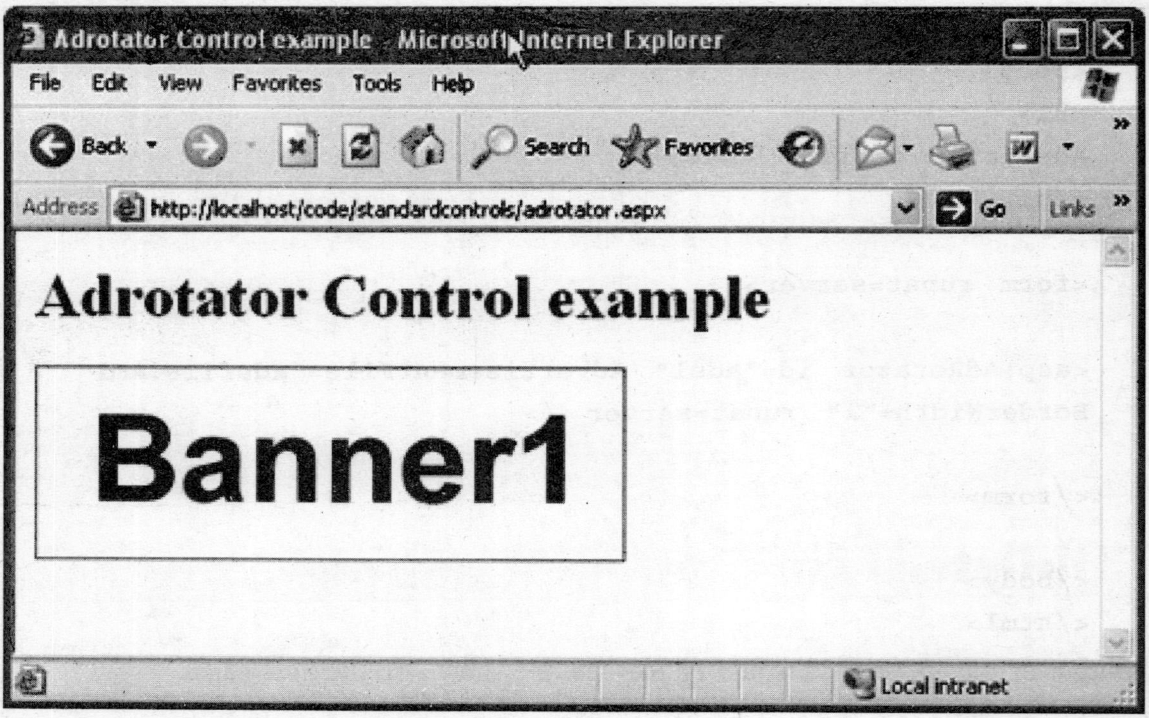


```
</title>
</head>

<body>
<h1>
BulletedList Control Example
</h1>

<form runat=server>

<asp:BulletedList  BulletStyle="square" runat=server>

   <asp:ListItem>Item First </asp:ListItem>
   <asp:ListItem>Item Second </asp:ListItem>
         <asp:ListItem>Item Third </asp:ListItem>
         <asp:ListItem>Item Fourth </asp:ListItem>
        </asp:BulletedList>
```

```
</form>

</body>
</html>
```

Output of the above code would be like this:

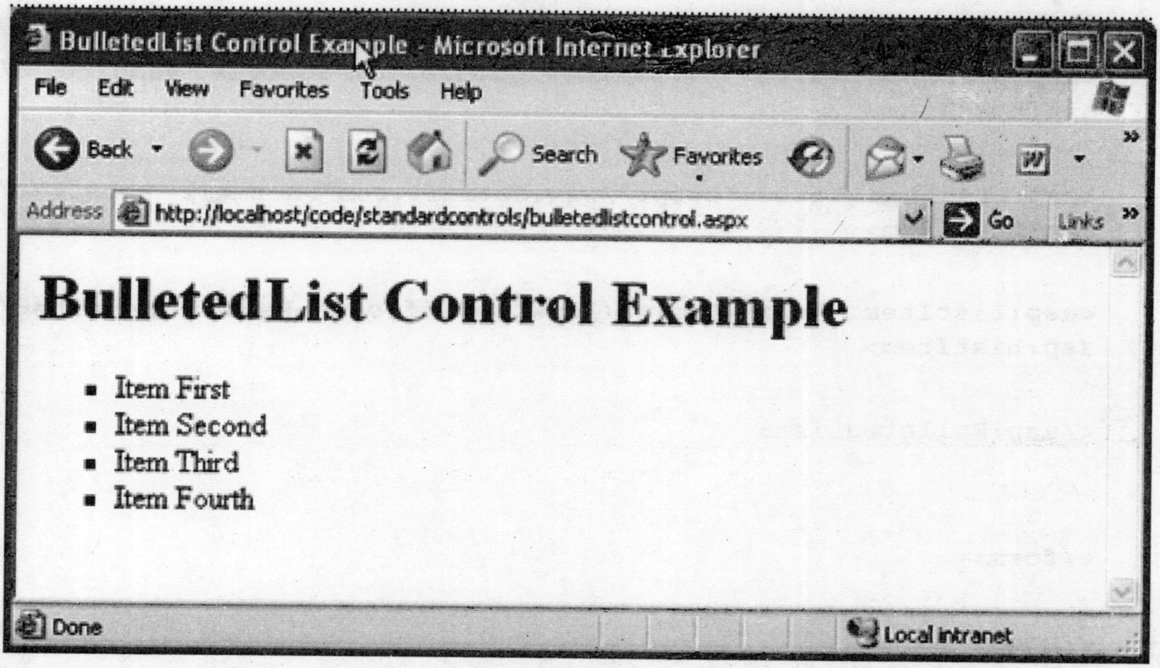

As I have explained you above that BulletedList control can also be render as a list of hyperlinks so below code will explain its implementation.

```
<html>
<head>
<title>
BulletedList Hyperlink Example
</title>
</head>

<body>
<h1>
BulletedList Hyperlink Example
</h1>
```

```
<form runat=server>

<asp:BulletedList DisplayMode = HyperLink runat=server>

<asp:ListItem Value="http://www.yahoo.com"> Yahoo Website </
asp:ListItem>

<asp:ListItem Value="http://www.google.com">Google Website </
asp:ListItem>

<asp:ListItem Value="http://www.hotmail.com">Hotmail Website</
asp:ListItem>

<asp:ListItem Value="http://www.rediff.com">Rediff Website</
asp:ListItem>

</asp:BulletedList>



</form>


</body>
</html>
```

Output of the above code would be like the one shown on the next page.

BUTTON CONTROL

This control behaves like a button as you see in Visual Basic or other languages. It is used to post a Web Forms page back to the server. Visitor simply clicks on it to perform certain actions.

For example:

```
<asp:Button Text="Submit" onclick="Button1_Click"
runat="server" />
```

The following code will explain the implementation of button control using ASP.Net 2.0

```
<html>
<head>
<title>
```

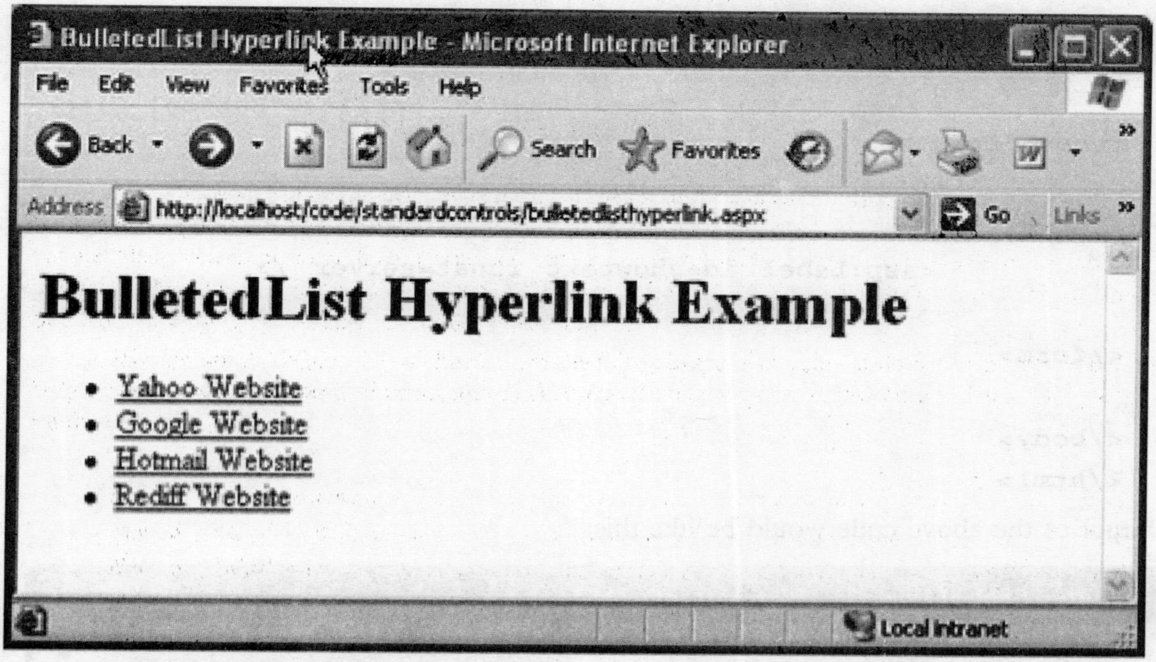


```
Button Control Example
</title>
<script language="VB" runat="server">

 Sub Button1_Click(sender As Object, e As EventArgs)

showtext.Text="Welcome to ASP.Net 2.0"

 End Sub

     </script>

</head>

<body>
<h1>
Button Control Example
</h1>
```

```
<form runat=server>

            <asp:Button  Text="Submit" onclick="Button1_Click"
runat="server" />
          <br>
   <br>
          <asp:Label id=showtext runat=server />

</form>

</body>
</html>
```

Output of the above code would be like this:

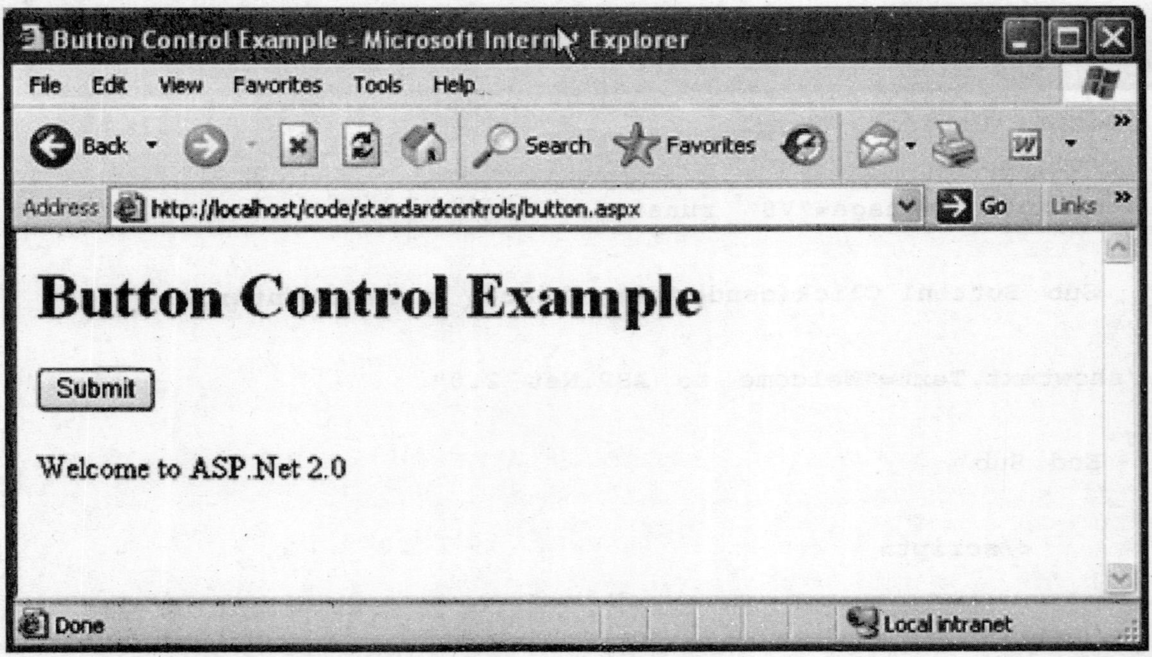

CALENDAR CONTROL

Calendar control is very important if you want to give users facility to select dates from your Web sites. It works just like Calendar. It displays a months from where visitors can select dates.

For example:

```
<asp:Calendar id=Calendar1 runat="server" />
```

Calendar control supports four types of date selection mode:

Mode	Description
Day	Visitor is able to select any single day.
DayWeek	Visitor is able to select an entire week or single day.
DayWeekMonth	Visitor is able to select a single day, an entire week, or the entire visible month.
None	In this mode date selection is always disabled.

The following will illustrate the implementation of Calendar Control:

```
<html>
<head>
<title>
Calendar Control Example
</title>
</head>

<body>
<h1>
Calendar Control Example
</h1>

<form runat=server>

<asp:Calendar id=Calendar1 runat="server"
              Height="220px" Width="350px"
              TitleStyle-BackColor="blue"
              TitleStyle-Font-Bold="True"
              TitleStyle-Font-Size="15px"
              SelectedDayStyle-BackColor="red"
              SelectedDayStyle-Font-Bold="True"
             />

</form>
```

```
</body>
</html>
```

Output of the above code would be like this:

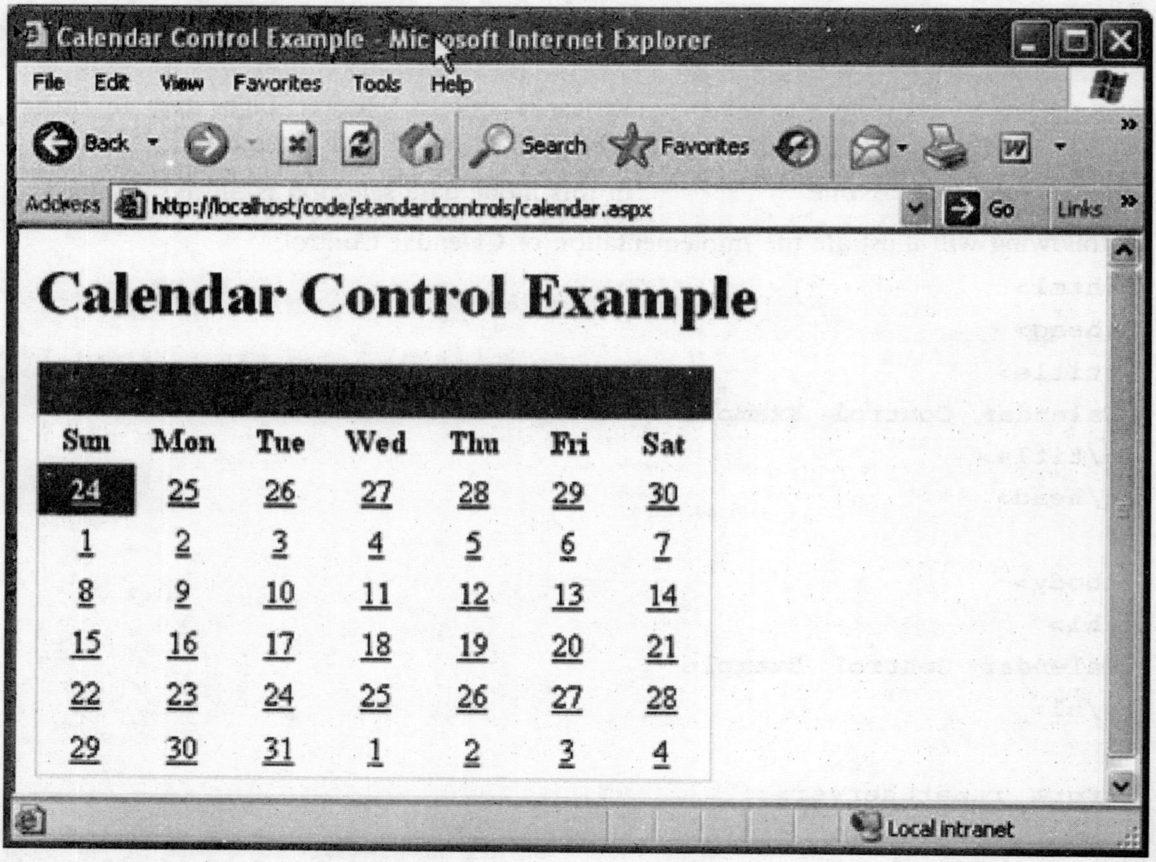

CHECKBOX CONTROL

This control is widely used in Website for making multiple selections. If visitor selects this property then its Checked property is set to True and if not then it will remain False.

For example:

```
<asp:CheckBox id=Checkbox1 runat="server" />
```

The following code will implement the use of Checkbox control:

```
<html>
<head>
<title>
Checkbox Control Example
```

```
</title>
 <script language="VB" runat="server">

        Sub validate_check(sender As Object, e As EventArgs)

            If Checkbox1.Checked = true Then

    showtext.Text = "Your hobby is Music"

            End If

  If Checkbox2.Checked = true Then

    showtext.Text = "Your hobby is Reading"

            End If

        End Sub
    </script>
</head>

<body>
<h1>
Checkbox Control Example
</h1>

<form runat=server>

<asp:CheckBox id=Checkbox1 Text="Music" runat="server" />
<asp:CheckBox id=Checkbox2 Text="Reading" runat="server" />

        <br>

            <asp:button text="Submit" OnClick="validate_check"
runat=server/>
```

```
<br>
<br>

            <asp:Label id=showtext   runat="server"/>

</form>

</body>
</html>
```

Output of the above code would be like this:

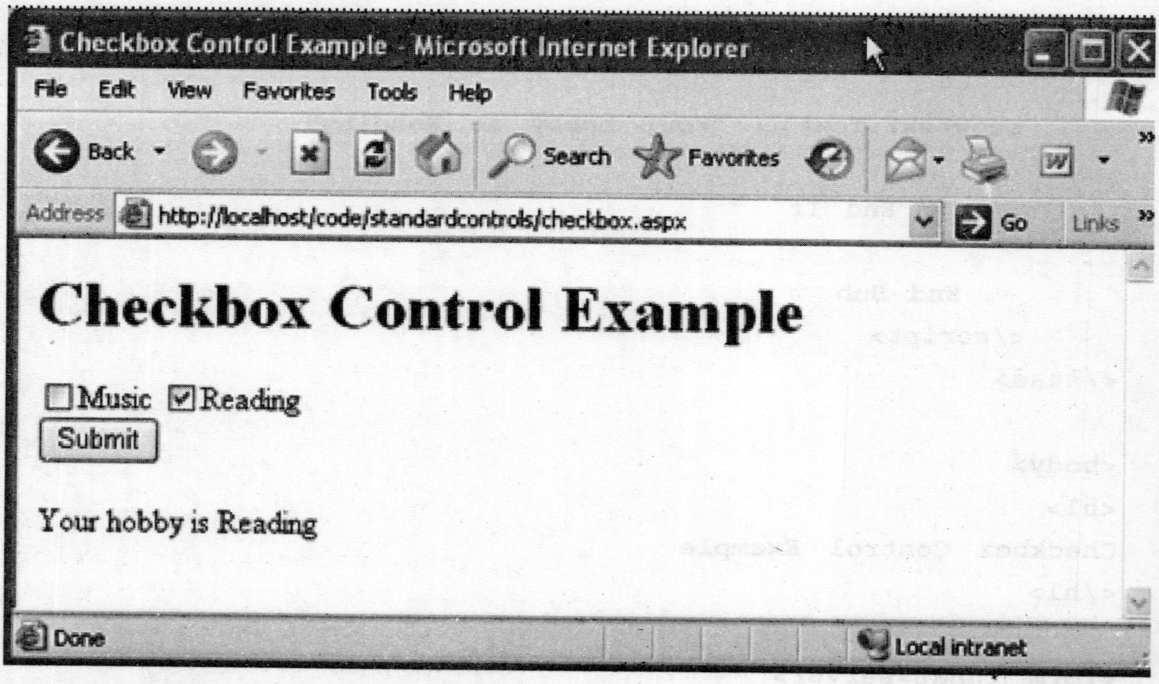

CHECKBOXLIST CONTROL

This control behaves same like a Checkbox control but only difference is it provides a multiple-selection checked list style. To identify the selected items you have to check the Selected property of an item.

For example:

```
        <asp:CheckBoxList  ID="Checkboxlist1"  runat="server">

           <asp:ListItem>Items..</asp:ListItem>
```

```
</asp:CheckBoxList>
```

The following code will explain the implementation of Checkboxlist control:

```
<html>
<head>
<title>
CheckBoxList Control Example
</title>
<script language="VB" runat="server">

Sub Proc_show(ByVal sender As Object, ByVal e As EventArgs)

Dim i As Integer
dim x as string

For i = 0 To Checkboxlist1.Items.Count - 1

If Checkboxlist1.Items(i).Selected Then
x = x & Checkboxlist1.Items(i).Text
x = x & "<br>"
End If

Next

        showtext.Text =  "You have selected following
items:<br><br>" & x

End Sub
</script>
</head>

<body>
<h1>
CheckBoxList Control Example
</h1>
```

```
<form runat=server>

     <asp:CheckBoxList ID="Checkboxlist1" runat="server">

          <asp:ListItem>Jan</asp:ListItem>
          <asp:ListItem>Feb</asp:ListItem>
          <asp:ListItem>Mar</asp:ListItem>
          <asp:ListItem>Apr</asp:ListItem>
          <asp:ListItem>May</asp:ListItem>
          <asp:ListItem>Jun</asp:ListItem>
          <asp:ListItem>Jul</asp:ListItem>
          <asp:ListItem>Aug</asp:ListItem>
          <asp:ListItem>Sept</asp:ListItem>
          <asp:ListItem>Oct</asp:ListItem>
          <asp:ListItem>Nov</asp:ListItem>
          <asp:ListItem>Dec</asp:ListItem>
 </asp:CheckBoxList>
<asp:Button  Text="Submit" OnClick="Proc_show" runat="server"
/>
 <asp:Label ID="showtext" runat="server" />

</form>

</body>
</html>
```

Output would be like the one shown on the next page.

DROPDOWNLIST CONTROL

This control is mostly used in Web sites, it provides the box in which you can add several items from where user or visitor can select one. In one time user can select one item from the list.

For example:

```
<asp:DropDownList id=DropDownlist1 runat="server">

 <asp:ListItem>Monday</asp:ListItem>
```

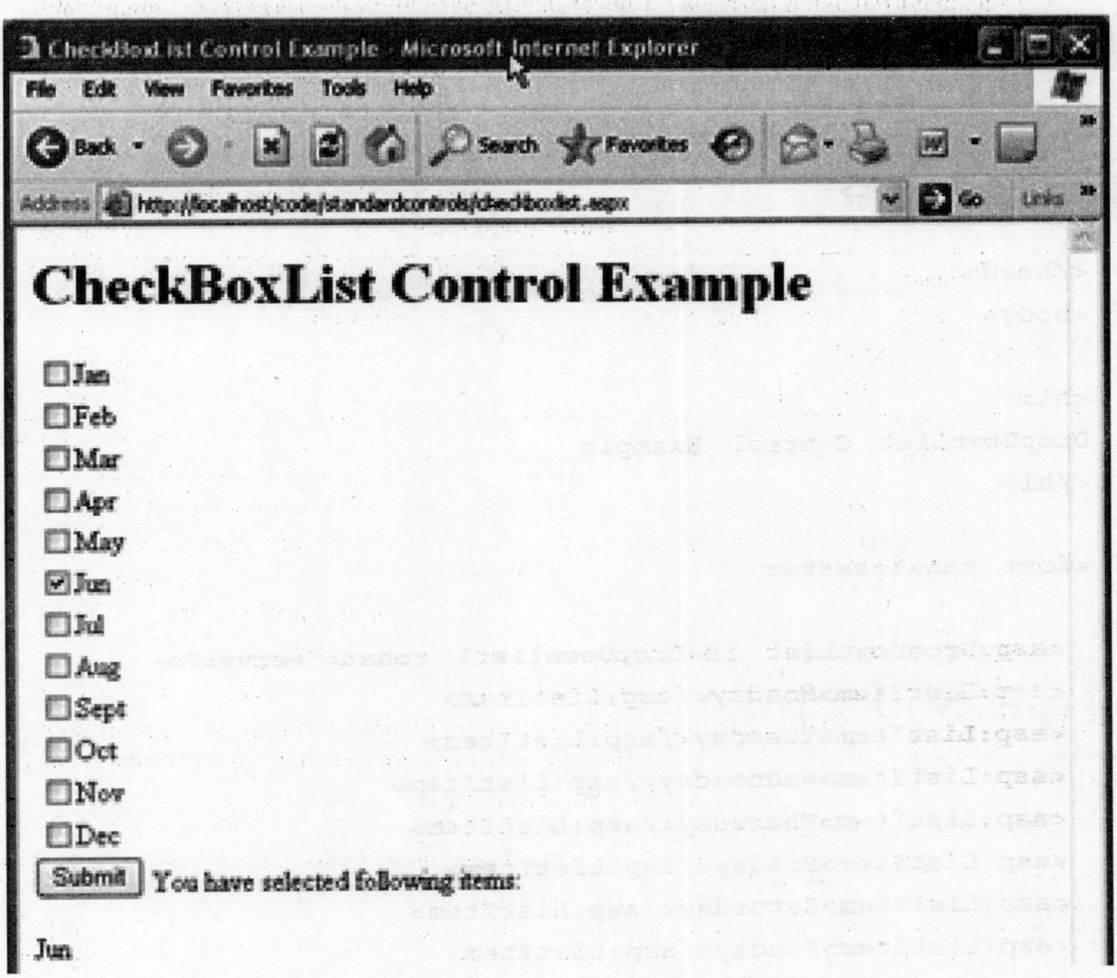


```
</asp:DropDownList>
```

The following code will implement the DropDownList control:

```
<html>
<head>
<title>
DropDownList Control Example
</title>

<script language="VB" runat="server">

        Sub Proc_show(sender As Object, e As EventArgs)
```

```
                    showtext.Text="<br><br>Day is: " +
DropDownlist1.SelectedItem.Text
          End Sub

     </script>

</head>
<body>

<h1>
DropDownList Control Example
</h1>

<form runat=server>

  <asp:DropDownList id=DropDownlist1 runat="server">
  <asp:ListItem>Monday</asp:ListItem>
  <asp:ListItem>Tuesday</asp:ListItem>
  <asp:ListItem>Wednesday</asp:ListItem>
  <asp:ListItem>Thursday</asp:ListItem>
  <asp:ListItem>Friday</asp:ListItem>
  <asp:ListItem>Saturday</asp:ListItem>
  <asp:ListItem>Sunday</asp:ListItem>
  </asp:DropDownList>

 <asp:button text="Click Me" OnClick="Proc_show" runat=server/
>
  <asp:Label id=showtext runat="server"/>

</form>

</body>
</html>
```

Output of the above code would be like this:

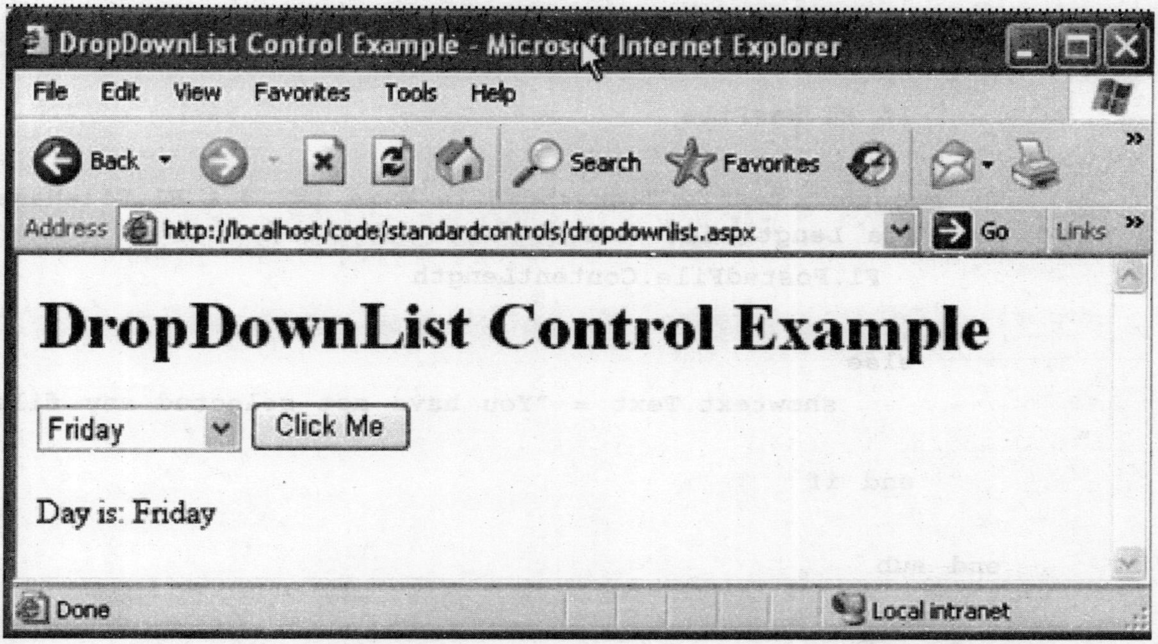

FILEUPLOAD CONTROL

Using FileUpload Control, users can upload the file to the Web Server. It is mostly used control for uploading the files.

For example:

```
<asp:FileUpLoad id="F1"  runat="server" />
```

Once the user has selected the file then you can upload it to Server using Save As property.

For example:

```
F1.SaveAs(F1.Filename)
```

This control provides Textbox and Browse button to locate the file.

Code:

```
<html>
<head>
<title>
Fileupload Control Example
</title>

 <script language="VB" runat="server">
```

```
    Sub run_proc(sender As Object, e As EventArgs)

            if F1.HasFile

         showtext.Text = "<br><br>File Name is: " & F1.FileName
& " and File Length is: " &
              F1.PostedFile.ContentLength

            else
                showtext.Text = "You have not selected any file
"
            end if

    end sub

    </script>

</head>
<body>

<h1>
Fileupload Control Example
</h1>

<form runat=server>

<asp:FileUpLoad id="F1"  runat="server" />

<asp:Button  Text="Upload" OnClick="run_proc" runat="server"
/>
<asp:Label id="showtext" runat="server" />

</form>

</body>
```

```
</html>
```

Output of the above code is like this:

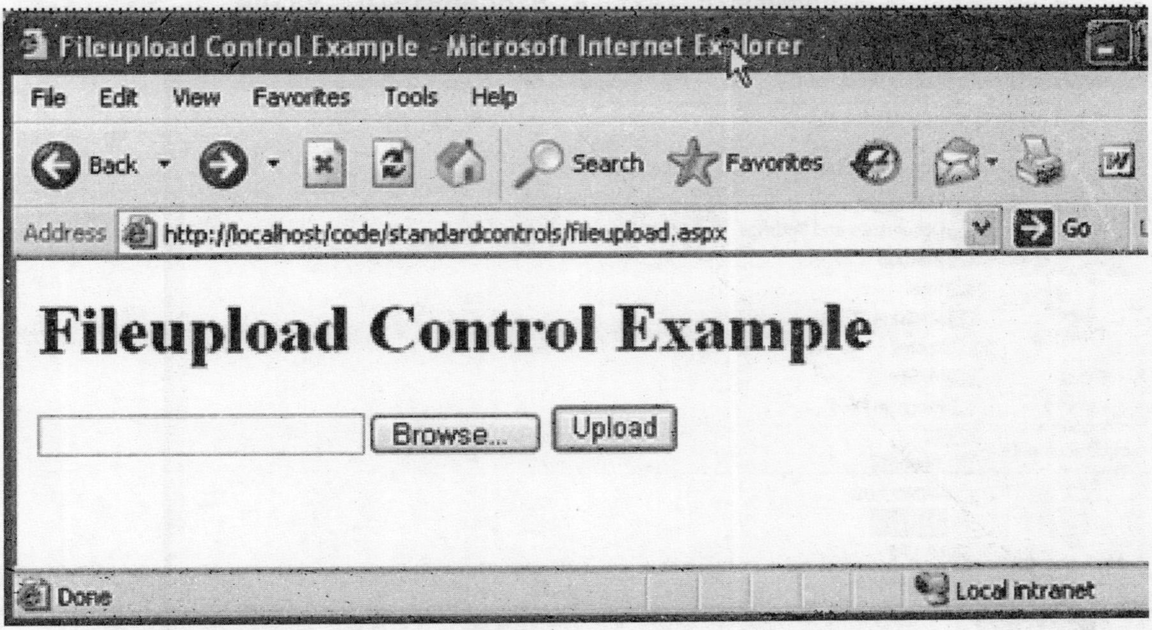

HIDDENFIELD CONTROL

If you want to store such values which you do not want to show the users then HiddenField control will solve your problem. Basically it persists the values from user to the server. HiddenField control is the best alternative if you do not want to use view state, cookies and session state. The negative point of HiddenField is they are not best meant for security issues. To store values inside HiddenField control you can use its Value property.

For example:

```
<asp:HiddenField id=HiddenField1 runat=Server />
```

The following code will show the implementation of HiddenField Control:

```
<html>
<head>
<title>
HiddenField Control Example
</title>

<script language="VB" runat="server">
```

```
Sub run_proc(sender As Object, e As EventArgs)
    HiddenField1.value = "Value 1"
    showtext.Text = HiddenField1.Value
```

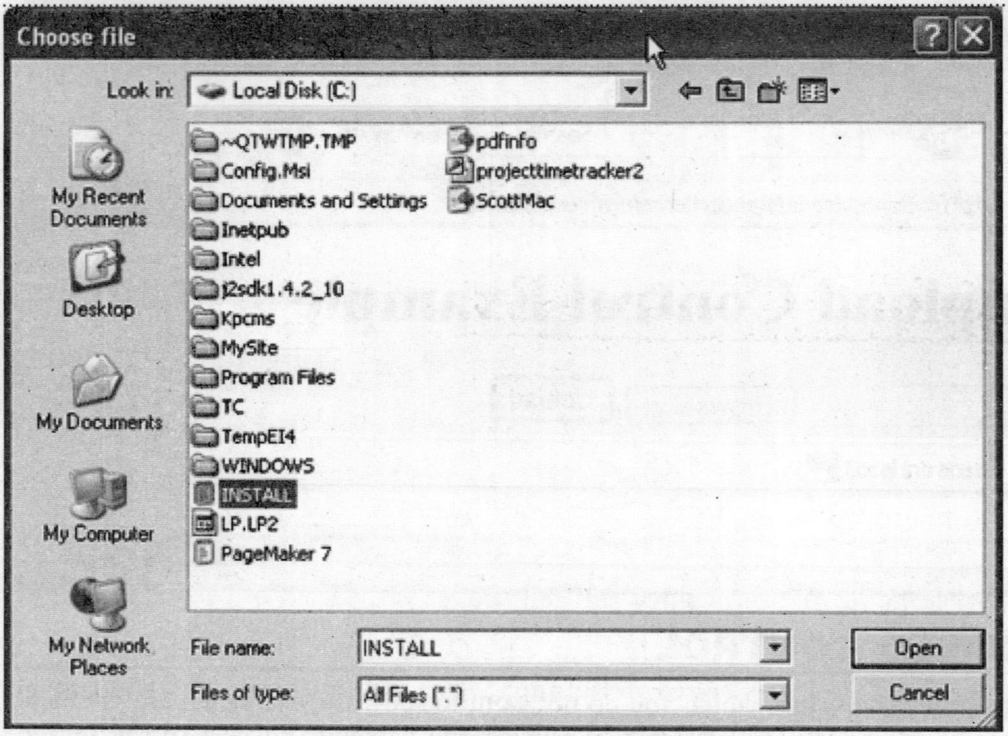

```
        End Sub

    </script>

</head>

<body>
<h1>
HiddenField Control Example
</h1>

<form runat=server>

<asp:HiddenField id=HiddenField1 runat=Server />
<asp:Button Text="Submit" onclick="run_proc" runat="server" /
>
<br>
<br>
<asp:label id="showtext" runat="Server" />

</form>

</body>
</html>
```

Output of the above code would be like the one shown on the next page.

HYPERLINK CONTROL

This control is used for the navigation purpose. It will navigate from one page to another page.

For example:

```
<asp:hyperlink id=HyperLink1 runat="server">
```

The following code will explain the implementation of Hyperlink control.

```
<html>
<head>
<title>
```

```
HyperLink Control Example
</title>

<script language="VB" runat="server">


    Sub Page_Load(sender As Object, e As EventArgs)

        HyperLink1.NavigateUrl = "http://www.yahoo.com"

    End Sub

</script>

</head>

<body>
<h1>
HyperLink Control Example
```

```
</h1>

<form runat=server>

  <asp:hyperlink id=HyperLink1 runat="server">
                 Click here
           </asp:hyperlink>

</form>

</body>
</html>
```

Output of the above code would be like this:

IMAGE CONTROL

The basic purpose of Image control is to display images. For this purpose you can use its ImageUrl property.

For example:

```
<asp:Image ImageUrl="imagepath.." runat="server" />
```

The following code will implement the Image control properly.

```
<html>
<head>
<title>
Image Control Example
</title>
</head>

<body>
<h1>
Image Control Example
</h1>

<form runat=server>

<asp:Image ImageUrl="banner1.gif" AlternateText="This is first
banner"
runat="server" />

</form>

</body>
</html>
```

Output of the above code would be like this:

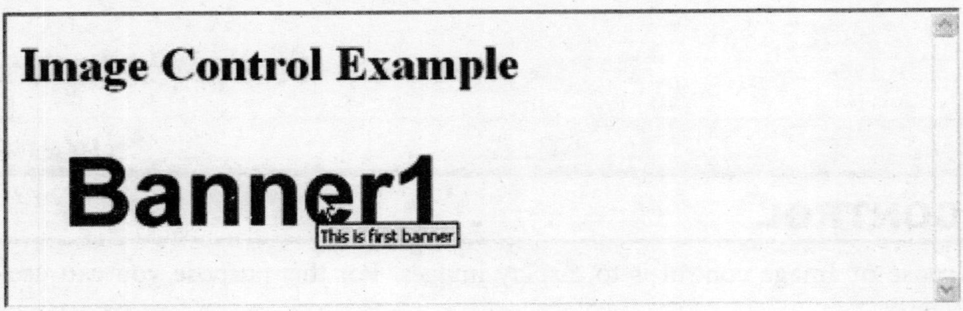

IMAGEBUTTON CONTROL

This control also displays the image but it behaves like a button control. It always post back to the server. You should always use ImageButton control if you want an functionality like this which displays the image too.

For example:

```
<asp:ImageButton id=ImageButton1 ImageUrl="imagelocation"
runat="server"/>
```

The following code will explain the implementation of ImageButton Control:

```
<html>
<head>
<title>
ImageButton Control Example
</title>
<script language="VB" runat="server">

            Sub run_proc(sender As Object, e As
ImageClickEventArgs)
            showtext.Text = "<br><br>Have you clicked the
Image button?"
        End Sub

    </script>
</head>
<body>

<h1>
ImageButton Control Example
</h1>

<form runat=server>

<asp:ImageButton id=ImageButton1 ImageUrl="banner1.gif"
BorderWidth="1px" onclick="run_proc" runat="server"/>

<asp:Label id=showtext runat=server />

</form>
```

```
</body>
</html>
```

Output of the above code would be like this:

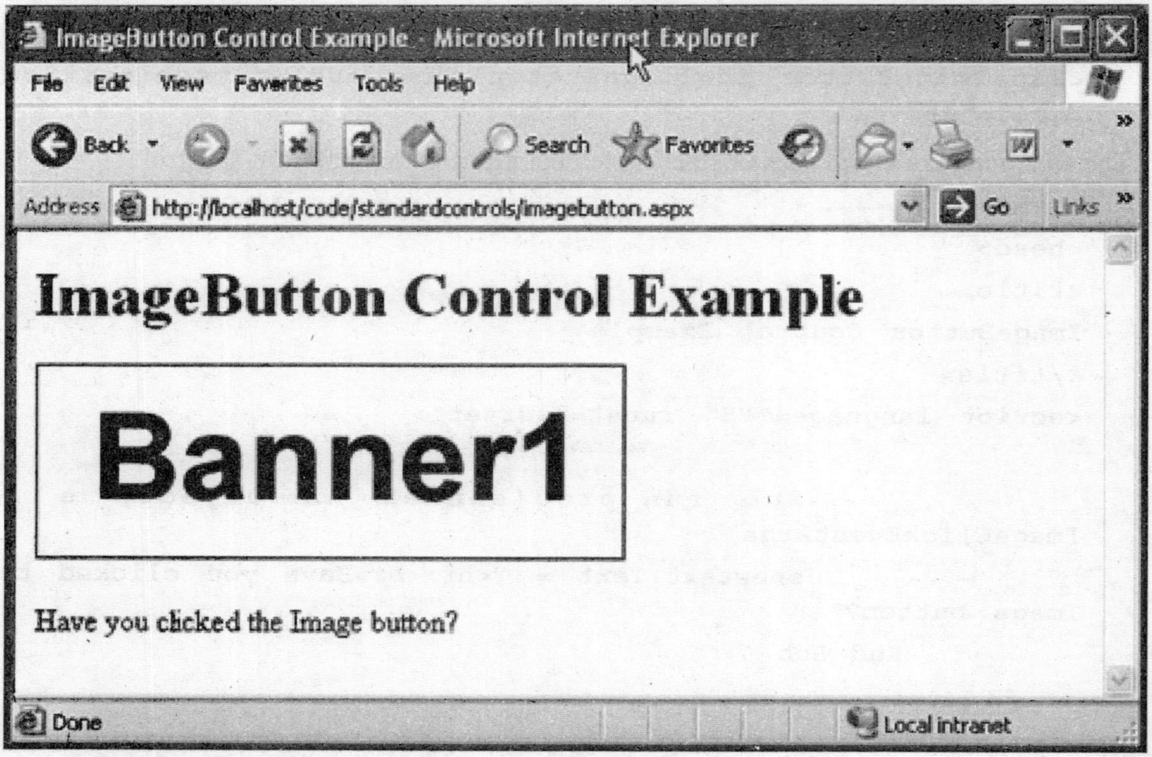

IMAGEMAP CONTROL

If you want to define hot spot regions on an image then for this purpose you can use ImagMap control. When user will click on the hot spot region he will be naviaged to the URL specified on hot spot region. You can also take use of this control to establish a post back to the server.

The following code will explain the ImageMap control's implementation:

```
<html>
<head>
<title>
ImageMap Control Example
</title>
</head>
```

```
<body>
<h1>
ImageMap Control Example
</h1>
<br>
First half of the image will navigate you to Contactus.html
and another half to feedback.html Web
page.
<br>
<form runat=server>

<asp:imagemap id="Buttons" imageurl="banner2.gif"
runat="Server">

                    <asp:RectangleHotSpot
                    hotspotmode="Navigate".
                    NavigateUrl="contactus.html"
                    alternatetext="Contact Us page"
                    top="0"
                    left="0"
                    bottom="100"
                    right="100">
                    </asp:RectangleHotSpot>

                    <asp:RectangleHotSpot
                    hotspotmode="Navigate"
                    NavigateUrl="feedback.html"
                    alternatetext="Feedback page"
                    top="0"
                    left="100"
                    bottom="100"
                    right="300">
                    </asp:RectangleHotSpot>

</asp:imagemap>
```

```
</form>

</body>
</html>
```

Output of the above code would be like this:

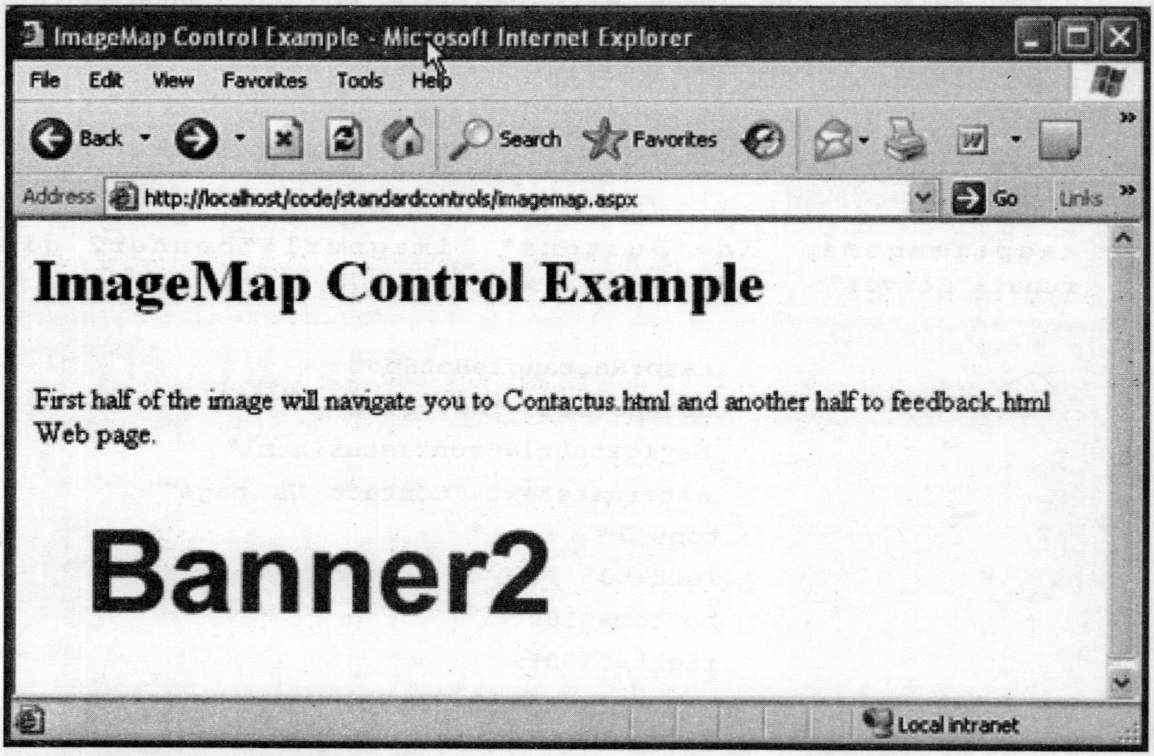

LABEL CONTROL

The basic purpose of Label control is to display text. You can show text using its Text property.

For example:

```
Label1.text = "Jasmin"
```

The following code will show the implementation of Label control:

```
<html>
<head>
<title>
Label Control Example
</title>
```

```
<script language="VB" runat="server">

        Sub run_proc(sender As Object, e As EventArgs)
                                        showtext.Text =
System.Web.HttpUtility.HtmlEncode(Textbox1.Text)
        End Sub

    </script>

</head>

<body>
<h1>
Label Control Example
</h1>

<form runat=server>

<asp:TextBox id="Textbox1" Text="" Width="300px" runat="server"
/>
<br>
<br>
<asp:Button   Text="Show on Label" OnClick="run_proc"
Runat="server"/>
<br>
<br>
<asp:Label id="showtext"  runat="server"/>

</form>

</body>
</html>
```

Output of the above code would be like this:

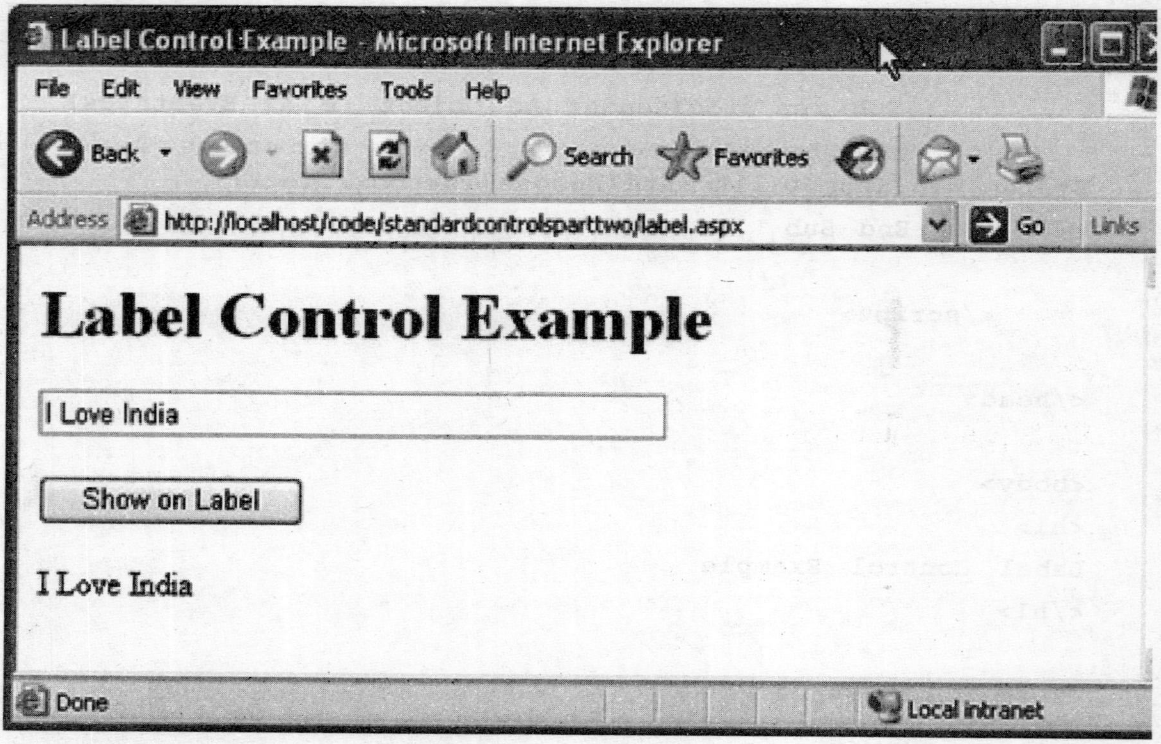

LINKBUTTON CONTROL

LinkButton control also behaves like a Button control. It is used to post a Web Forms page back to the server

For example:

```
<asp:LinkButton Text="Some text..." onclick="Procedure to
execute.." runat="server"/>
```

The following code will explain the implementation of LinkButton control.

```
<html>
<head>
<title>
LinkButton Control Example
</title>
<script language="VB" runat="server">

        Sub run_proc(sender As Object, e As EventArgs)
              showtext.Text="Thanks for clicking!"
        End Sub
```

```
    </script>

</head>

<body>
<h1>
LinkButton Control Example
</h1>

<form runat=server>

<asp:LinkButton Text="Just Click Here" onclick="run_proc"
runat="server"/>

<br>
<br>

<asp:Label id=showtext runat=server />

</form>
</body>
</html>
```

Output of the above code would be like the one shown on the next page. The first figure shows before clicking and the second one shows after clicking.

LISTBOX CONTROL

ListBox control is used to select value. It has a single or multiple selection list style. You have seen ListBox control mostly in registration forms because it saves the space. If you wish to have ListBox control in mutiple-selection mode then for this purpose set its SelectionMode property to Multiple.

For example:

```
<asp:ListBox    runat="server">
        <asp:ListItem>Items....</asp:ListItem>
        <asp:ListItem> Items....</asp:ListItem>
      </asp:ListBox>
```

The following code will explain the implementation of ListBox control:

```
<html>
<head>
```

```
<title>
Listbox Control Example
</title>
</head>

<body>
<h1>
Listbox Control Example
</h1>

<form runat=server>

 <asp:ListBox    runat="server">

          <asp:ListItem>India</asp:ListItem>
          <asp:ListItem>USA</asp:ListItem>
          <asp:ListItem>Australia</asp:ListItem>
          <asp:ListItem>Japan</asp:ListItem>
          <asp:ListItem>China</asp:ListItem>
          <asp:ListItem>Bangladesh</asp:ListItem>

        </asp:ListBox>

</form>

</body>
</html>
```

Output of the above code would be like the one shown on the next page.

LITERAL CONTROL

Its basic purpose is to display the text. Literal control always passes the content directly to the Web browsers. You cannot apply the styles to literal control.

For example:

```
<asp:Literal  Text="Some text..." runat=server />
```

The following code will explain the implementation of Literal Control.

```
<html>
<head>
<title>
Literal Control Example
</title>
</head>

<body>
<h1>
Literal Control Example
</h1>

<form runat=server>

<asp:Literal  Text="This text is gerenated by literal control"
runat=server />

</form>
```

```
</body>
</html>
```

Output of the above code would be like this:

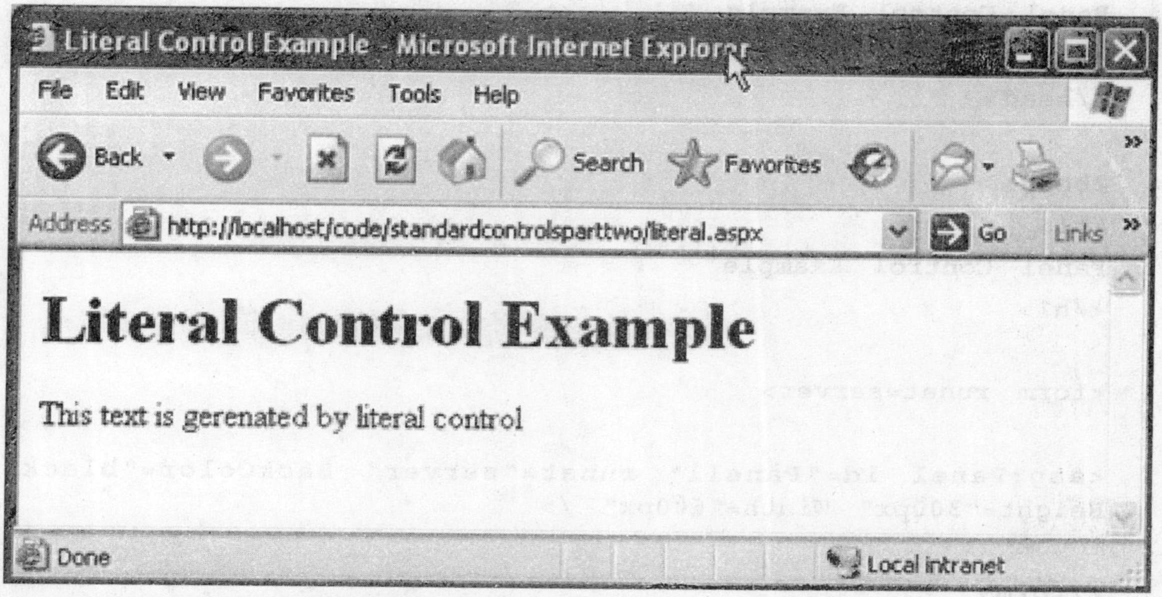

MULTIVIEW CONTROL

This is a container control for groups of View controls. Here every View control will contain child controls.

For example:

```
<asp:MultiView ID="MV1" runat="server" ActiveViewIndex="0">
 <asp:View ID="V1" runat="server">
 This is View<br><br>
 <asp:label ID="showtext" runat="server"></asp:TextBox>
</asp:View>
</asp:MultiView>
```

PANEL CONTROL

This control acts like a container for other ASP.Net controls. This control is much more handled through code.

For example:

```
<asp:Panel id="Panel1" runat="server">
```

The following code will show the implementation of Panel control:

```
<html>
<head>
<title>
Panel Control Example
</title>
</head>

<body>
<h1>
Panel Control Example
</h1>

<form runat=server>

<asp:Panel id="Panel1" runat="server" BackColor="black"
Height="300px" Width="600px" />

</form>

</body>
</html>
```

Output of the above code would be like the one shown on the next page.

PLACEHOLDER CONTROL

This control also acts like a container control but it dynamically loads other controls. You can add controls dynamically during execution.

For example:

```
<asp:PlaceHolder id="Placeholder1" runat="server" />
```

The following code will show the implementation of PlaceHolder Control:

```
<html>
<head>
<title>
PlaceHolder Control Example
</title>
<script language="VB" runat="Server">
```

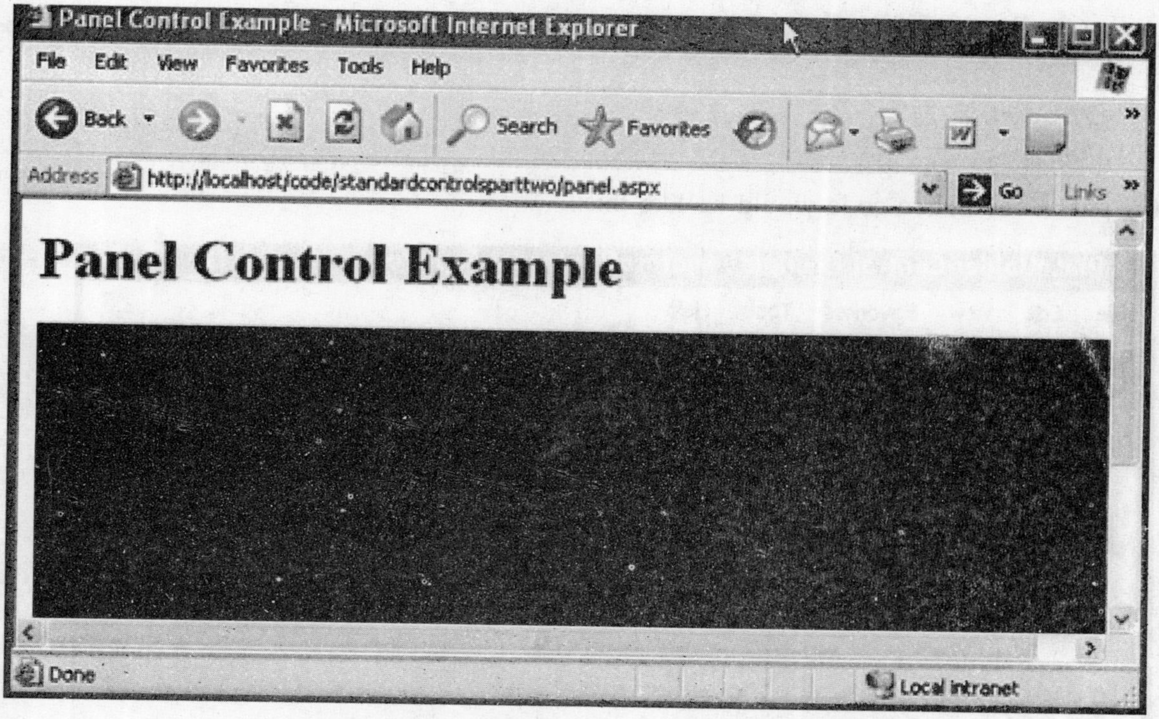


```
Sub Page_Load(Sender As Object, E As EventArgs)
Dim txtb As Textbox = New Textbox()
        txtb.Text = "I Love India"
        Placeholder1.Controls.Add(txtb)

End Sub
</script>
</head>

<body>
<h1>
PlaceHolder Control Example
</h1>

<form runat=server>

<asp:PlaceHolder id="Placeholder1" runat="server" />
```

```
</form>

</body>
</html>
```

Output of the above code would be like this:

RADIOBUTTON CONTROL

If from the range of selection you want to give a choice to user to select one item then Radio button will sort out your problem. To group several buttons into one you should give them same name.

For example:

```
<asp:RadioButton Id=Radiocontrol1 Text="some text"
GroupName="RadioGroup1" runat="server"/>
```

The following code will show the implementation of RadioButton control.

```
<html>
<head>
<title>
Radio Control Example
</title>
  <script language="VB" runat="server">
```

```
Sub run_proc(sender As Object, e As EventArgs)

  If Radiocontrol1.Checked Then
  showtext.Text = "Your choice is: " & Radiocontrol1.Text
  Else If Radiocontrol2.Checked Then
  showtext.Text = "Your choice is: " & Radiocontrol2.Text
  End If

End Sub

    </script>

</head>

<body>
<h1>
Radio Control Example
</h1>

<form runat=server>

<asp:RadioButton id=Radiocontrol1 Text="Science" Checked="False"
GroupName="RadioGroup1" runat="server" />
<asp:RadioButton id=Radiocontrol2 Text="Maths" Checked="True"
GroupName="RadioGroup1" runat="server" />
<asp:button text="Submit" OnClick="run_proc" runat=server/>

<Br>
<Br>

<asp:Label id=showtext  runat="server" />

</form>

</body>
```

```
</html>
```

Output of the above code would be like this:

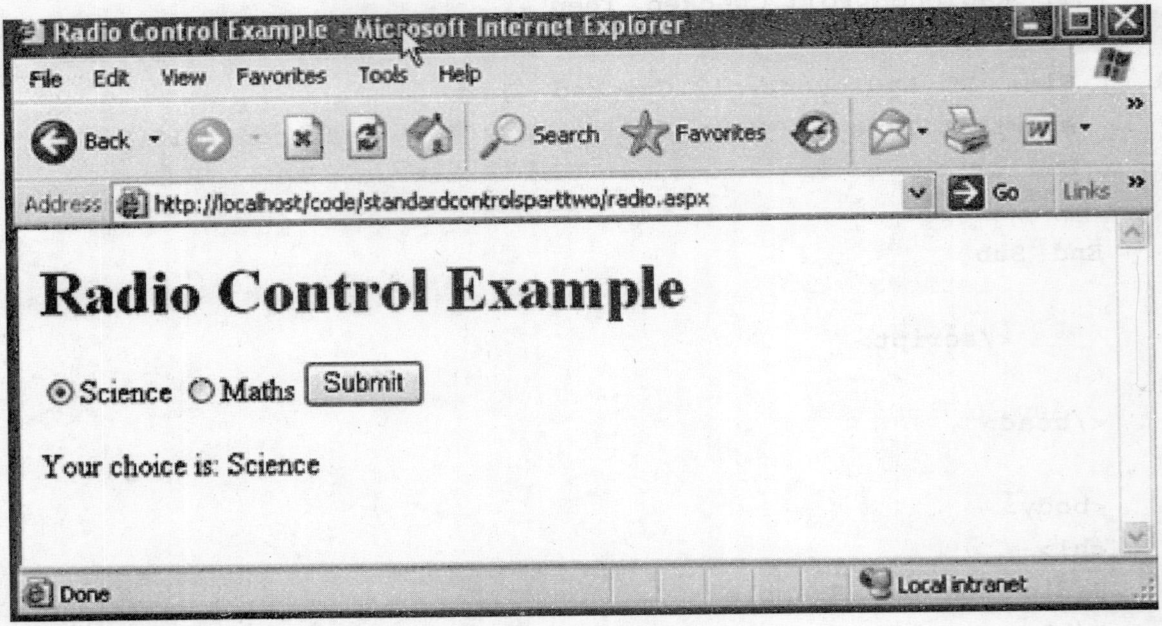

RADIOBUTTONLIST CONTROL

This control also acts like a Radio control but only difference is it provides a single-selection checked list. For manipulation of items we have its Items collection To identify the selected items you have to check the Selected property of an item..

For example:

```
<asp:RadioButtonList id=Radiobuttonlistcontrol1 runat="server">
   <asp:ListItem>Some Item...</asp:ListItem>
</asp:RadioButtonList>
```

The following code will show the implementation of RadioButtonList control:

```
<html>
<head>
<title>
RadioButtonList Control Example
</title>
</head>

<body>
```

```
<h1>
RadioButtonList  Control  Example
</h1>
<form  runat=server>
<asp:RadioButtonList id=Radiobuttonlistcontroll runat="server">

<asp:ListItem>Cricket</asp:ListItem>
<asp:ListItem>Tennis</asp:ListItem>
<asp:ListItem>Football</asp:ListItem>
<asp:ListItem>Rugby</asp:ListItem>
<asp:ListItem>BAsketball</asp:ListItem>

</asp:RadioButtonList>

</form>

</body>
</html>
```

Output of the above code would be like the one shown on the next page.

SUBSTITUTION CONTROL

This control is used for the substitution of content. You have to set the MehtodName property of Substitution server control to static method on the control.

For example:

```
<asp:Substitution  ID="Substitutioncontrol1"  runat="Server"  />
```

The following code will show the implementation of Substitution control:

```
<html>
<head>
<title>
Substitution  Control  Example
</title>
<script  language  =  "VB"  runat="server">

     Shared Function run_proc(ByVal  context  As  HttpContext)  As
String
```

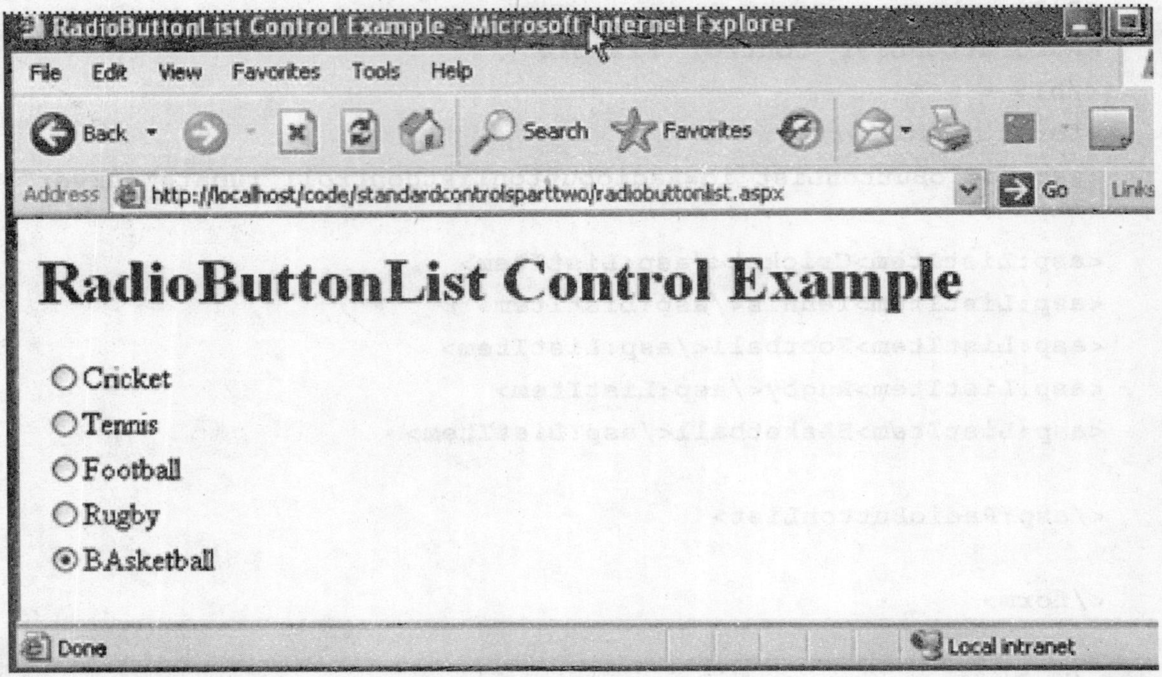


```
        Return "Learning ASP.Net 2.0"
    End Function

</script>
</head>

<body>
<h1>
Substitution Control Example
</h1>

<form runat=server>

<asp:Substitution  MethodName="run_proc"  runat="server"  />

</form>

</body>
</html>
```

Output of the above control would be like this:

TABLE CONTROL

This control is used for building Tables. You already have used <Table> tag in HTML. Here you generate the table programmatically. To add content to a table cell you can add controls to the Controls collection of the cell.

For example:

```
<asp:Table id="Tablecontrol1" CellPadding=2 CellSpacing=3
BorderWidth="2" BorderColor="blue" Gridlines="Both"
runat="server"/>
```

TEXTBOX CONTROL

You have seen this control almost in registration forms. It is used for taking input from user or visitor. You can also set the behavior of Textbox control as Multiline or Password type but for this you have to set the TextMode property of Textbox control to Multiline or Password.

For example:

```
<asp:Textbox ID="Textboxcontrol1" runat="Server">
```

The following code will show the implementation of Textbox control.

```
<html>
```

```
<head>
<title>
Textbox Control Example
</title>
<Script language="VB" runat="Server" >
Sub run_proc(Sender As Object, E As EventArgs)
showtext.text = Textboxcontrol1.text
End Sub
</Script>
</head>
<body>
<h1>
Textbox Control Example
</h1>
<form runat=server>
<asp:Textbox ID="Textboxcontrol1" runat="Server" />
<br>
<asp:Button Text="Click Me" OnClick="run_proc" runat="Server"
/>
<br>
<br>
<asp:label ID="showtext" runat="Server" />
</form>
</body>
</html>
```

Output of the above code would be like the one shown on the next page.

WIZARD CONTROL

The basic purpose of this control is to provide navigations. It will give you series of steps and as an input it takes information from the visitor or user.

User can see the content through Wizardstep where as at one time only one Wizardstep can be displayed.

For example:

```
<asp:Wizard ID="Wizardcontrol1" runat="server" >
    <WizardSteps>
```

```
<asp:WizardStep Title="First step of Wizard "runat="server" >
  </asp:WizardStep>

</WizardSteps>
</asp:Wizard>
```

XML CONTROL

XML control is used for two purposes:

1. To write the result of an XSL Transform.
2. To write an XML document.

To specify the XML document you can use DocumentSource property.

For example:

```
<asp:Xml id="xmlcontrol1" DocumentSource="xml file ..."
TransformSource="xsl file..." runat="server" />
```

The following code will show the implementation of XML control:

```
<html>
<head>
<title>
```

```
XML Control Example
</title>
</head>
<body>
<h1>
XML Control Example
</h1>
<form runat=server>

<asp:Xml id="xmlcontrol1" DocumentSource="xmlfile.xml"
TransformSource="xslfile.xsl"
runat="server" />

</form>
</body>
</html>
```

Besides these codes, there are some HTML controls which are useful in ASP. They are shown next with examples.

HTMLANCHOR CONTROL

The basic purpose of HtmlAnchor control is in navigation. It takes you from one Web page to another.

For example:

```
<a id=anchor1 href= "some link..." runat="server">
                    Text to show...
             </a>
```

The following code will show the implementation of HtmlAnchor Control:

```
<html>
<head>
<title>
HtmlAnchor Control Example
</title>
</head>

<body>
```

```
<h1>
HtmlAnchor Control Example
</h1>

<form runat=server>

<a id=anchor1 href= "http://www.yahoo.com" runat="server">
                Click here
            </a>


</form>
</body>
</html>
```

Output of the above code would be like this:

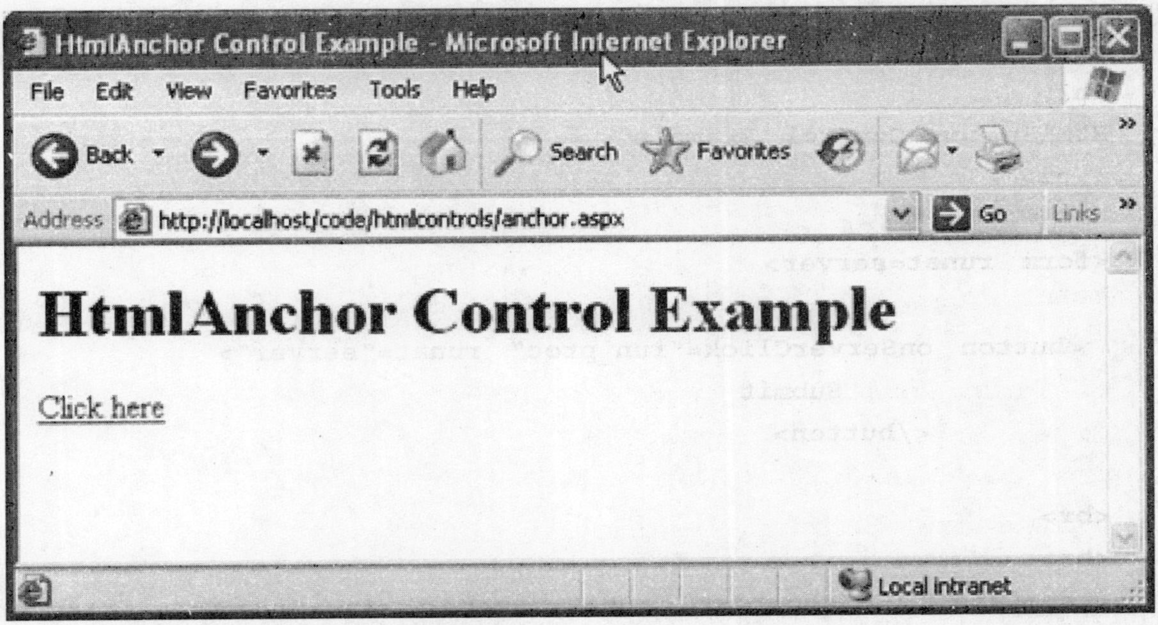

HTMLBUTTON CONTROL

It behaves like a button. Whenever user will click on this button you can run some code according to business logic. You can run the procedure or function declared inside the script.

For example:

```
<button id=Bn onServerClick="procedure to execute"
runat="server">
```

```
                Submit
            </button>
```

The following code will show the implementation of Button control:

```
<html>
<head>
<title>
HtmlButton Control Example
</title>
<script language="VB" runat="server">
sub run_proc(sender as object, e as eventargs)
showtext.text = "Button has been clicked"
end sub
</script>
</head>

<body>
<h1>
HtmlButton Control Example
</h1>

<form runat=server>

  <button onServerClick="run_proc" runat="server">
                Submit
            </button>


<br>
<br>
<asp:Label ID="showtext" runat="server" />
</form>

</body>
</html>
```

Output would be like the one shown on the next page.

HTMLFORM CONTROL

Its major use is to process postback activities. All textbox, button etc controls reside inside a HtmlForm control so that information should be send easily to server without any troubles using Get or Post methods.

```
<html>
<head>
<title>
HtmlForm Control Example
</title>
<script language="VB" runat="server">
         Sub run_proc(sender As Object, e As EventArgs)
               showtext.InnerHtml = "Yeah you have clicked
HTMLButton Control"
         End Sub
  </script>
</head>

<body>
<h1>
HtmlForm Control Example
```

```
</h1>
<form runat=server>

        <input onServerClick="run_proc" value=" Click Me"
type="submit"   runat="server" >
<br>
<br>
<span id=showtext runat=server />

  </form>

</body>
</html>
```

Output of the above code would be like this:

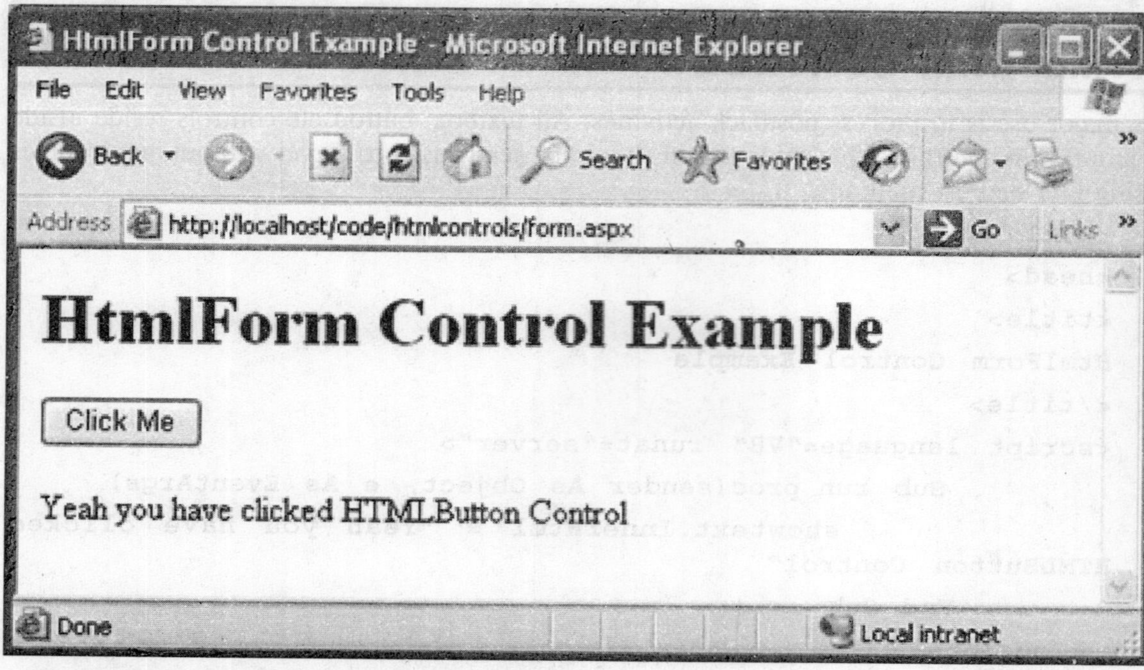

HTMLGENERIC CONTROL

There are few controls like <body>. <div> etc which are not directly used by HTML server control. So HtmlGeneric controls is an best alternative to use them.

For example:

```
pagebody.Attributes("bgcolor") = choosecolor.Value
```

The following code will show the implementation of HtmlGeneric control:

```
<html>
<head>
<title>
HtmlGeneric Control Example
</title>
<script language="VB" runat="server">

     Sub run_proc(sender As Object, e As EventArgs)
          pagebody.Attributes("bgcolor") = choosecolor.Value
     End Sub

</script>
</head>

<body id="pagebody" runat="server">

<h1>
HtmlGeneric Control Example
</h1>

<form runat=server>

<select id="choosecolor" runat="server">
            <option>Yellow</option>
            <option>Green</option>
   </select>
       <input Value="Click here" type="submit"
OnServerClick="run_proc" runat="server" >

</form>

</body>
</html>
```

Output of the above code would be like this:

HTMLIMAGE CONTROL

This control is used to display the image. For this you can use its Src property.

For example:

```
<img src="image path..." runat="server"/>
```

The following code will show the implementation of HtmlImage Control:

```
<html>
<head>
<title>
HtmlImage Control Example
</title>
</head>

<body>
<h1>
HtmlImage Control Example
</h1>

<form runat=server>
```

```
<img  src="banner3.gif"  runat="server"/>
</form>

</body>
</html>
```

Output of the above code would be like this:

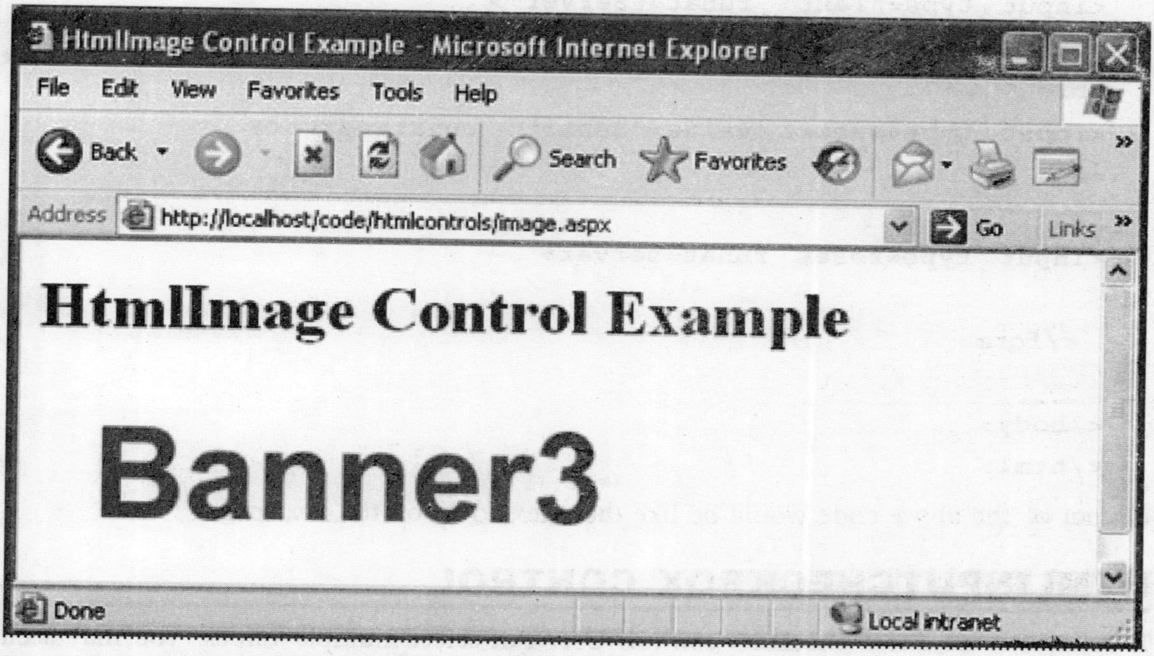

HTMLINPUTBUTTON CONTROL

This control can target any browser. It behaves same like button control.

The following code will show the implementation of HtmlInputButton control:

```
<html>
<head>
<title>
HtmlInputButton  Control  Example
</title>

</head>

<body>
```

```
<h1>
HtmlInputButton Control Example
</h1>

<form runat=server>

<input type="Text" runat="Server">
<br>
<br>
<input type=submit value="Submit" runat=server>
<br>
<br>
<input type=reset runat=server>

  </form>

</body>
</html>
```

Output of the above code would be like the one shown on the next page.

HTMLINPUTCHECKBOX CONTROL

It behaves same like a checkbox control. User can select multiple values. You may seen this control mostly in registration forms.

For example:

The following code will show the implementation of HtmlInputCheckbox control:

```
<html>
<head>
<title>
HtmlInputCheckbox Example
</title>

<script language="VB" runat="server">

  Sub run_proc(sender As Object, e As EventArgs)
```

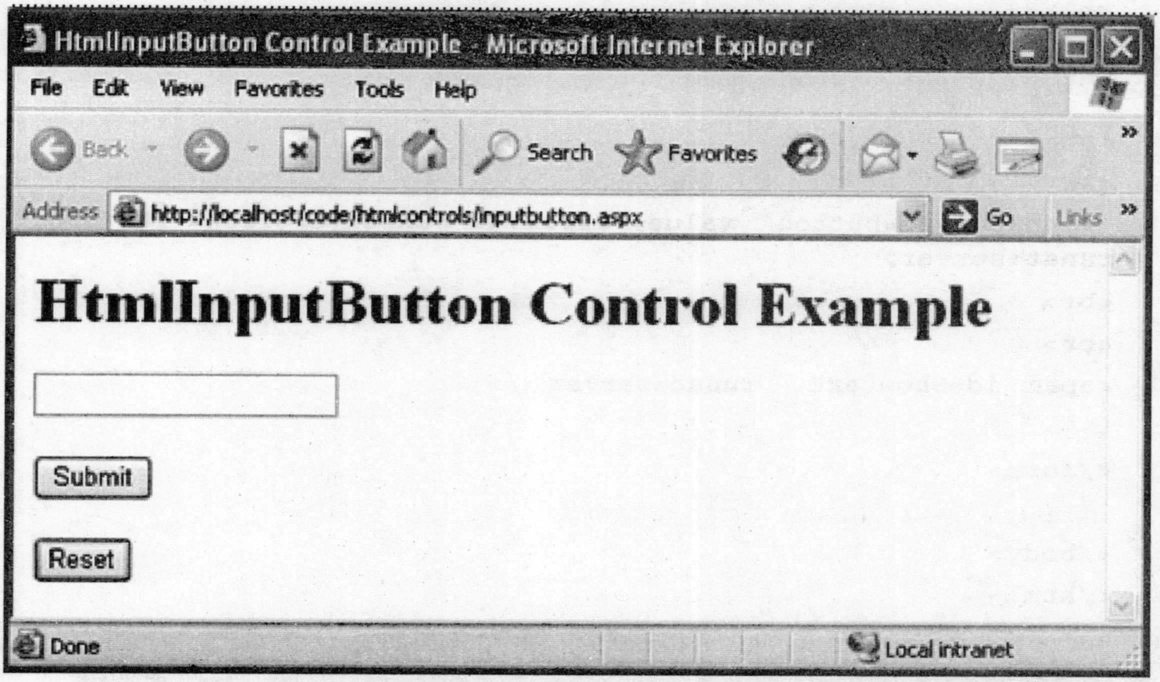


```
    If Checkboxcontrol1.Checked Then
                  Showtext.InnerHtml = "You like Cricket"
         Else
                Showtext.InnerHtml = "You do not like Cricket"
      End If
  End Sub

      </script>

</head>

<body>
<h1>
HtmlInputCheckbox Example
</h1>

<form runat=server>
```

```
<input id="Checkboxcontrol1" type=checkbox runat="server">
Cricket

<br>
<br>
 <input type=button  value="Click Me" OnServerClick="run_proc"
runat=server>
<br>
<br>
<span id=Showtext  runat=server />

</form>

</body>
</html>
```

Output of the above code would be like this:

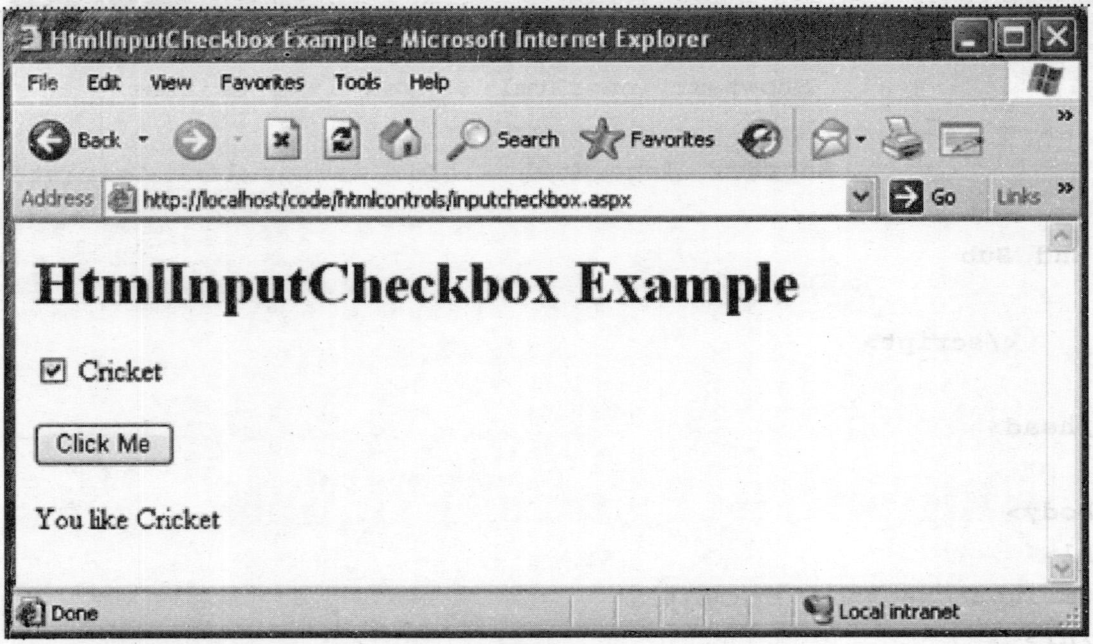

HTMLINPUTFILE CONTROL

This control is useful when you want to give such facility in Web site so that user can upload files to Web Server.

The following code will show the example:

```
<html>
<head>
<title>
HtmlInputFile  Control  Example
</title>
</head>
<body>
<h1>
HtmlInputFile  Control  Example
</h1>
<form  runat=server>
<input   type=file  runat="server">
<Br>
<Br>
<input  type=button   value="Upload  File"   runat="server">
</form>
</body>
</html>
```

Output of the above code would be like this:

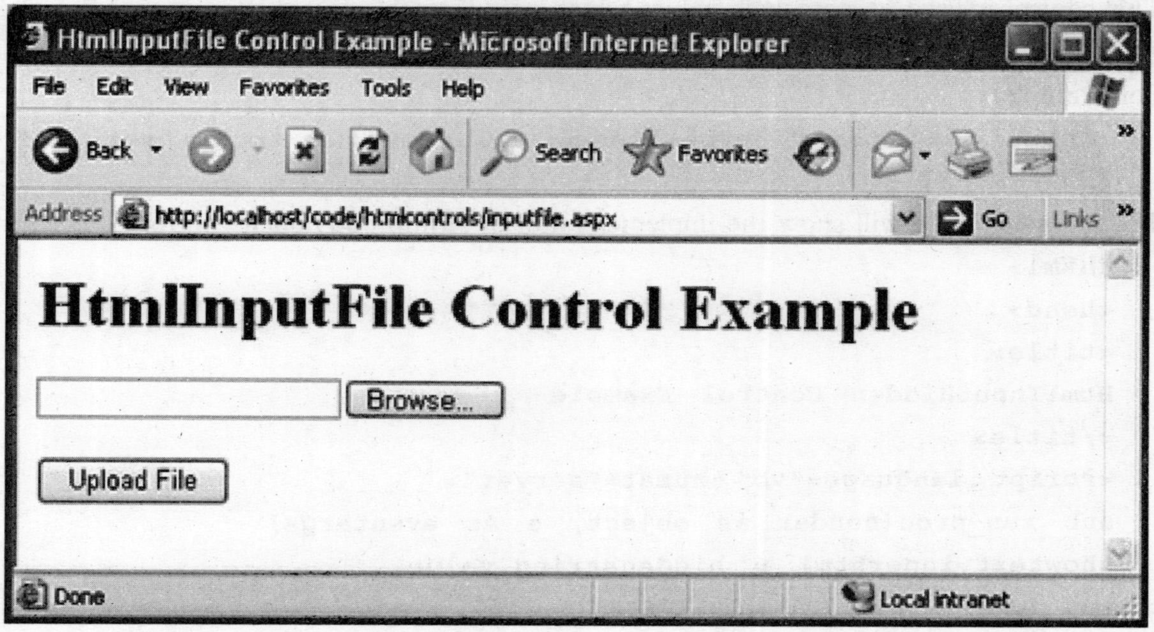

If user will click on Browse button following dialog box will appear to select the file for uploading:

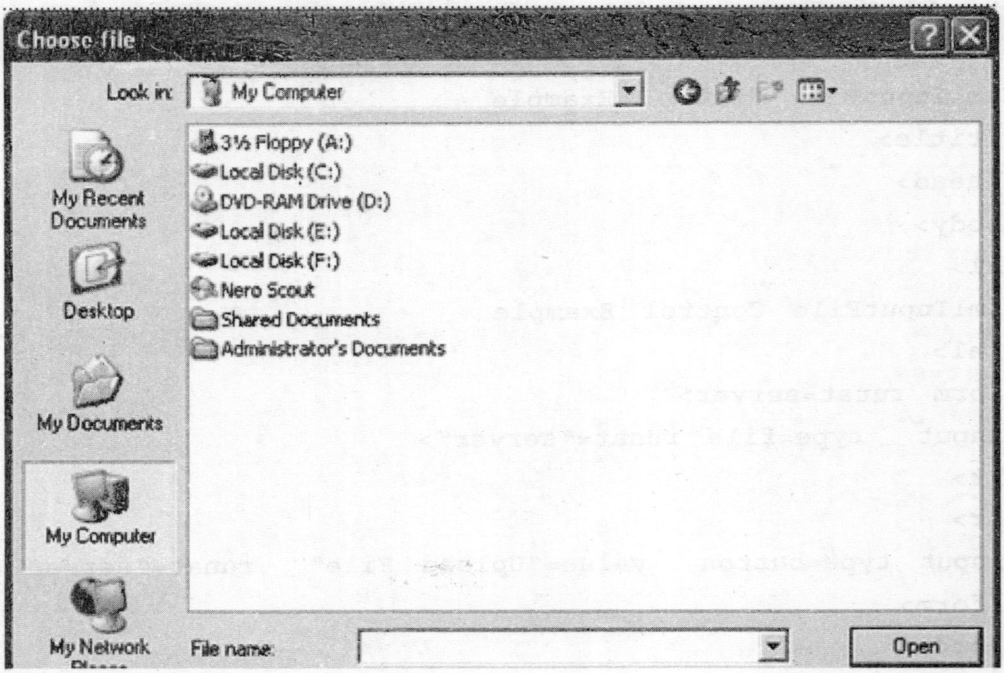

HTMLINPUTHIDDEN CONTROL

This control is used to store such values which user is unable to see. You can send such values in hidden way to server.

For example:

```
<input id="name.." type=hidden value="value to be set...."
runat=server>
```

The following code will show the implementation of HtmlInputHidden control:

```
<html>
<head>
<title>
HtmlInputHidden Control Example
</title>
<script language="vb" runat="server">
sub run_proc(sender as object, e as eventargs)
showtext.innerhtml = hiddenstring.value
end sub
```

```
</script>
</head>

<body>
<h1>
HtmlInputHidden Control Example
</h1>

<form runat=server>

<input id="Hiddenstring" type=hidden value="userform"
runat=server>
<input type="button" value="click me" onserverclick="run_proc"
runat="server" >
<br>
<br>
Hidden value is:
<span id="showtext" runat="server" ></span>

</form>

</body>
</html>
```

Output of the above code would be like the one shown on the next page.

HTMLINPUTIMAGE CONTROL

This control is used when you want that displaying image should act like a button control. Alternatively you can say this that this control is a button control with image.

For example:

```
<input type=image src="image path.." onserverclick="procedure
to execute.." runat="server">
```

The following code will show the implementation of HtmlInputImage control:

```
<html>
<head>
<title>
```

```
HtmlInputImage Control Example
</title>
<script langauge="vb" runat="server">
sub run_proc(sender as object, e as imageclickeventargs)
showtext.innerhtml = "Button control has been clicked"
end sub
</script>
</head>

<body>
<h1>
HtmlInputImage Control Example
</h1>

<form runat=server>
        <input   type=image              src="banner3.gif"
onserverclick="run_proc" runat="server">
<br>
<br>
<span id="showtext" runat="Server"></span>
</form>
```

```
</body>
</html>
```

Output of the above code would be like this:

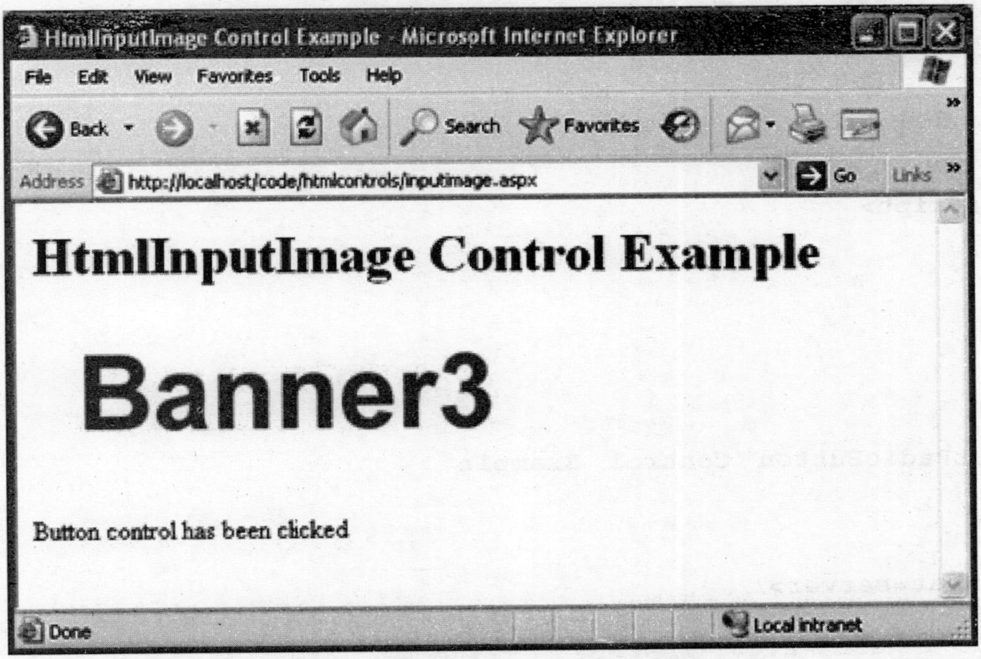

HTMLINPUTRADIOBUTTON CONTROL

This control is used when you want to give such control to user so that he/she can select single option from group of multiple options. For this the name property of control should be same of all HtmlInputRadioButton controls.

For example:

```
<input type="radio" id="Radiocontrol1" name="radiogroup"
runat="server"/>
```

The following code will show the implementation of HtmlInputRadioButton Control:

```
<html>
<head>
<title>
HtmlInputRadioButton Control Example
</title>
  <script language="VB" runat="server">
```

```
        Sub run_proc(sender As Object, e As EventArgs)
            If Radiocontrol1.Checked = True Then
                Showtext.InnerHtml = "You like Pizza!"
          else
                Showtext.InnerHtml = "You like Burger!"
            End If
        End Sub

    </script>

</head>

<body>
<h1>
HtmlInputRadioButton Control Example
</h1>

<form runat=server>

<input type="radio" id="Radiocontrol1" name="radiogroup"
runat="server"/>Pizza
<br>
<input type="radio" id="Radiocontrol2" name="radiogroup"
runat="server"/>Burger
<br>
<br>
   <span id=showtext runat=server />
<br>
<br>
  <input type=button id="Button1" value="Click Here"
OnServerClick="run_proc" runat=server>

</form>

</body>
```

```
</html>
```

Output of the above code would be like this:

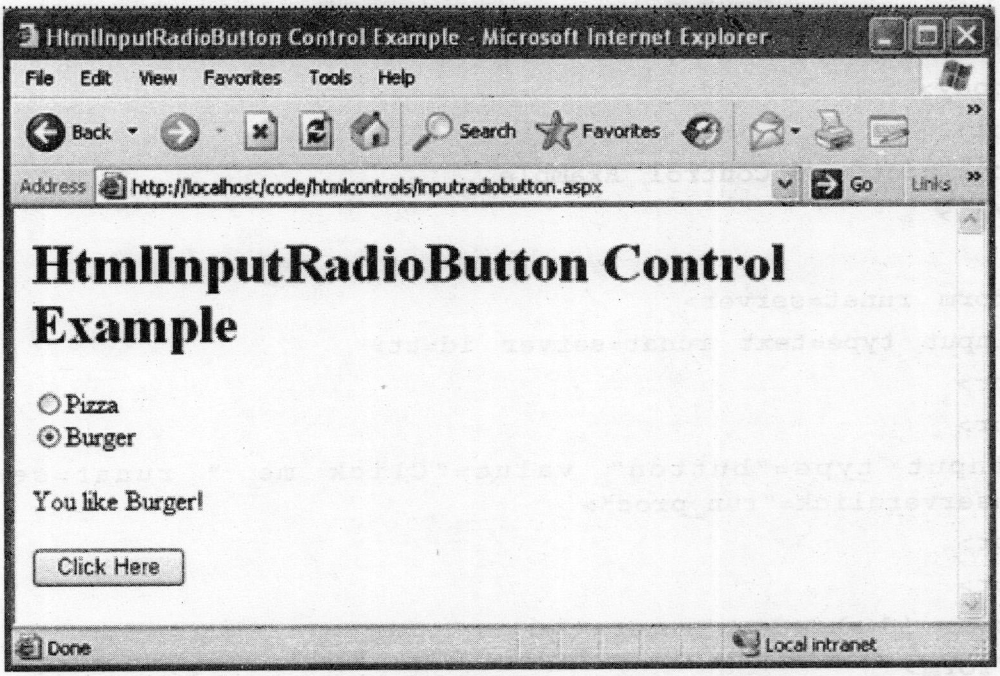

HTMLINPUTTEXT CONTROL

As name suggests using this control user can input the information as a text. Text can be anything combination of letters, numbers etc. This control can be also used as a password type for this you have to set the type property as password.

For normal textbox control you can use following syntax:

```
<input type=text runat = server id="name of the control">
```

The following code will show the implementation of HtmlInputText control:

```
<html>
<head>
<title>
HtmlInputText Control Example
</title>

<script language="vb" runat="Server">
sub run_proc(sender as object, system as eventargs)
showtext.innerhtml = "You have entered: " & tt.value
```

```
end sub
</script>

</head>
<body>
<h1>
HtmlInputText Control Example
</h1>

<form runat=server>
<input type=text runat=server id=tt>
<br>
<br>
<input type="button" value="Click me " runat=server
onserverclick="run_proc">
<br>
<br>
<span id=showtext runat="Server" />
</form>
</body>
</html>
```

Output of the above code would be like this:

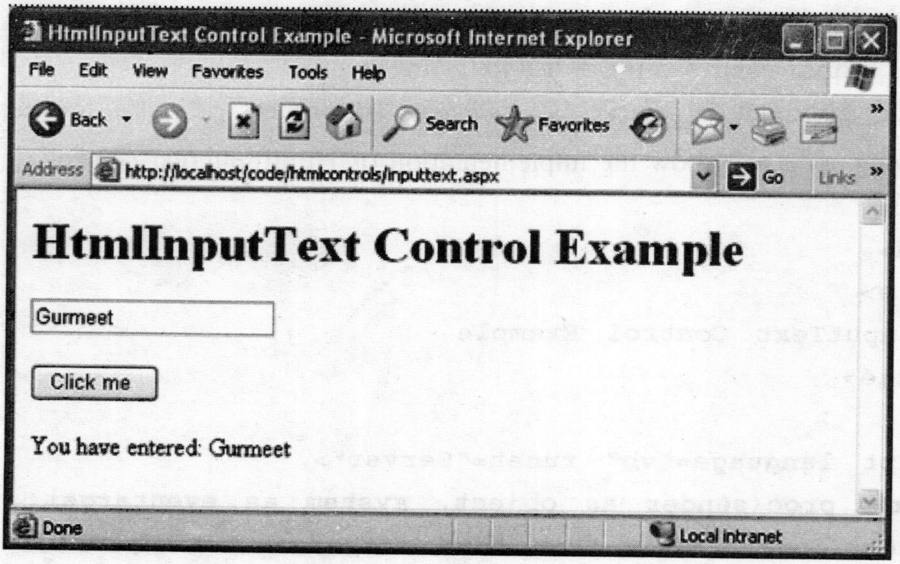

As I have explained above that you can also use this control as a password type. You may noticed such control in registration form where actual text is not visible while typing and replaced with * on the time of typing password.

For this you can use such syntax:

```
<input type=password runat=server id=password>
```

The following code will explain the implementation of this control as a password type:

```
<html>
<head>
<title>
Password Type Control  Example
</title>
<script language="vb" runat="Server">
sub run_proc(sender as object, system as eventargs)
showtext.innerhtml = "You have entered: " & tt.value
end sub
</script>
</head>
<body>
<h1>
Password Type Control Example
</h1>
<form runat=server>
<input type=password runat=server id=tt>
<br>
<br>
<input type="button" value="Click me " runat=server
onserverclick="run_proc">
<br>
<br>
<span id=showtext runat="Server" />
</form>
</body>
</html>
```

Output of the above code would be like this:

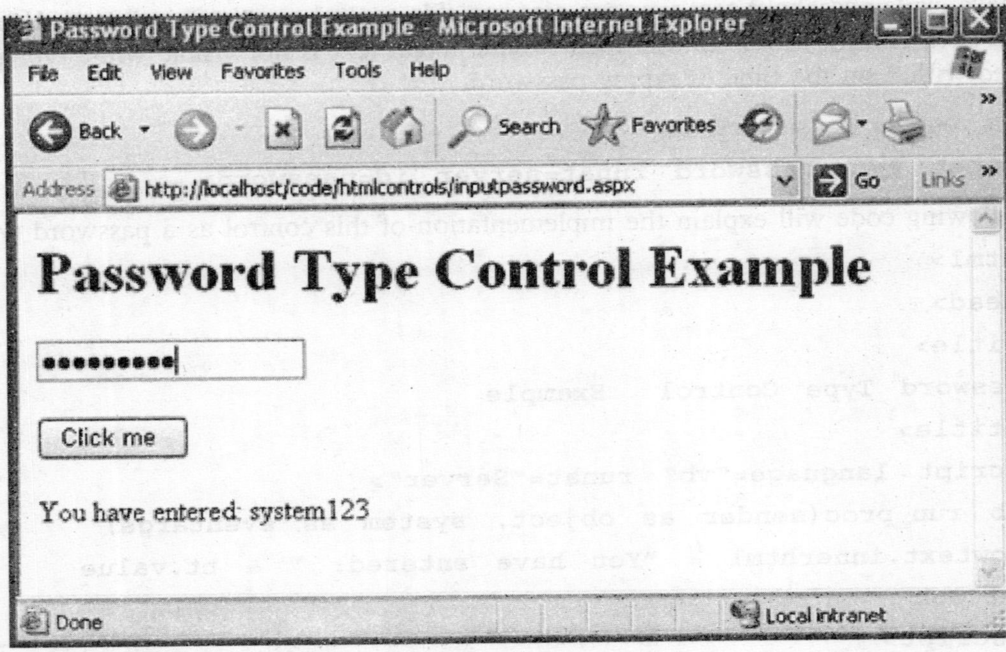

HTMLSELECT CONTROL

This is a drop-down type of control from where user can select one item or value. This control saves lot of space.

For example:

```
<select id="nameofcontrol" runat="server">
<option> first </option>
<option> second </option>
......
</select>
```

The following code will show the implementation of HtmlSelect control:

```
<html>
<head>
<title>
HtmlSelect Control Example
</title>
<script language="vb" runat="Server">
sub run_proc(sender as object, e as eventargs)
showtext.innerhtml = "You have selected:= " &
selectcontrol.value & " Country"
```

```
end sub
</script>
</head>
<body>
<h1>
HtmlSelect Control Example
</h1>
<form runat=server>
<select id="selectcontrol" runat="server">
   <option>India</option>
   <option>USA</option>
   <option>UK</option>
</select>
<br>
<Br>
<input type="button" value="Click Me" runat="server"
onserverclick="run_proc">
<Br>
<br>
<span id=showtext  runat="Server" />
</form>
</body>
</html>
```

Output of the above code would be like the one shown on the next page.

HTMLTABLE CONTROL

This control behaves like a table tag of HTML. This adds the table to your Web page programmatically. For this it adds the HtmlTableCell control to the row's cells collection and HtmlTableRow controls to the table's row collection.

For example:

```
<textarea id="control name" cols=60 rows=10 runat=server />
```

The following code will show the implementation of HtmlTextArea control:

```
<html>
<head>
<title>
```

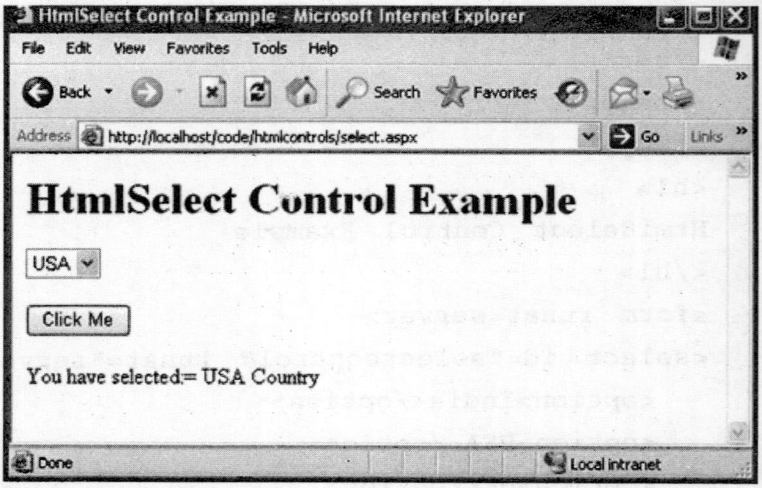


```
HtmlTextArea Control Example
</title>
</head>
<body>
<h1>
HtmlTextArea Control Example
</h1>
<form runat=server>
<textarea id="TextAreaControl1" cols=60 rows=10 runat=server
/>
</form>
</body>
</html>
```

Output of the above code would be like this:

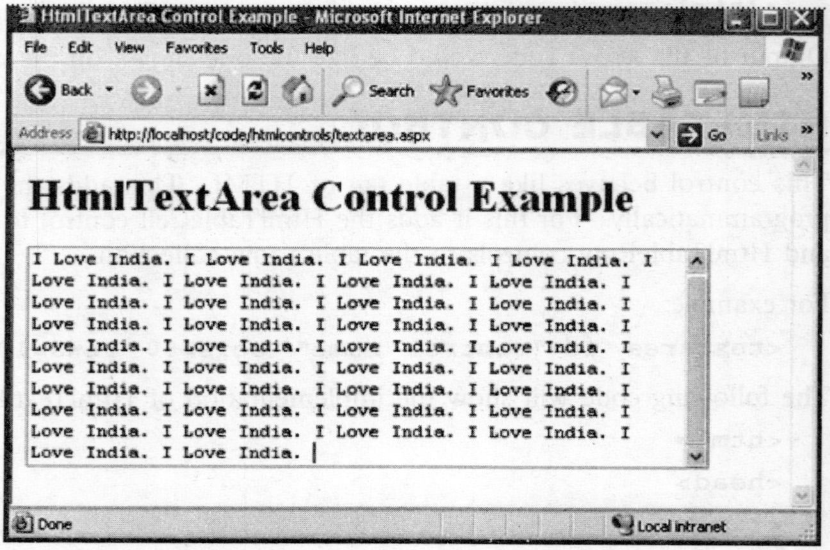

3 Other Controls of ASP

REQUIREDFIELDVALIDATOR CONTROLS

If you want that user should enter some values for example in Textbox control then for this you need to write some script. Previously you do this using JavaScript or VbScript at client side. But now you do not need to write such scripts. ASP provides built-in functionality for this. You just need to type a single line of code to validate the control. Just bind the RequiredFieldValidation control with the control which you want to validate using ControlToValidate property. ReuiredFieldValidator control forces user to enter some value.

For example:

```
<asp:RequiredFieldValidator id="RequiredFieldValidator1"
ControlToValidate="name of the control which you want to
validate..." runat="server">
```

Here you type the error message which you want to display!

```
</asp:RequiredFieldValidator>
```

The followng code will show the implementation of RequiredFieldValidator Control:

```
<html>
<head>
<title>
RequiredFieldValidator Control Example
</title>
</head>

<body>
<h1>
RequiredFieldValidator Control Example
</h1>

<form runat=server>

<asp:RequiredFieldValidator id="RequiredFieldValidator1"
ControlToValidate="Textboxcontrol1" runat="server">
```

```
 You must enter the value, Error!
</asp:RequiredFieldValidator>
<br>
Please Enter Your Name: <asp:TextBox id=Textboxcontrol1
runat="server"/>
<br>
<br>
<asp:Button Text="Click Here" runat="Server"
onserverclick="run_proc" />

</form>

</body>
</html>
```

Output of the above code would be like this:

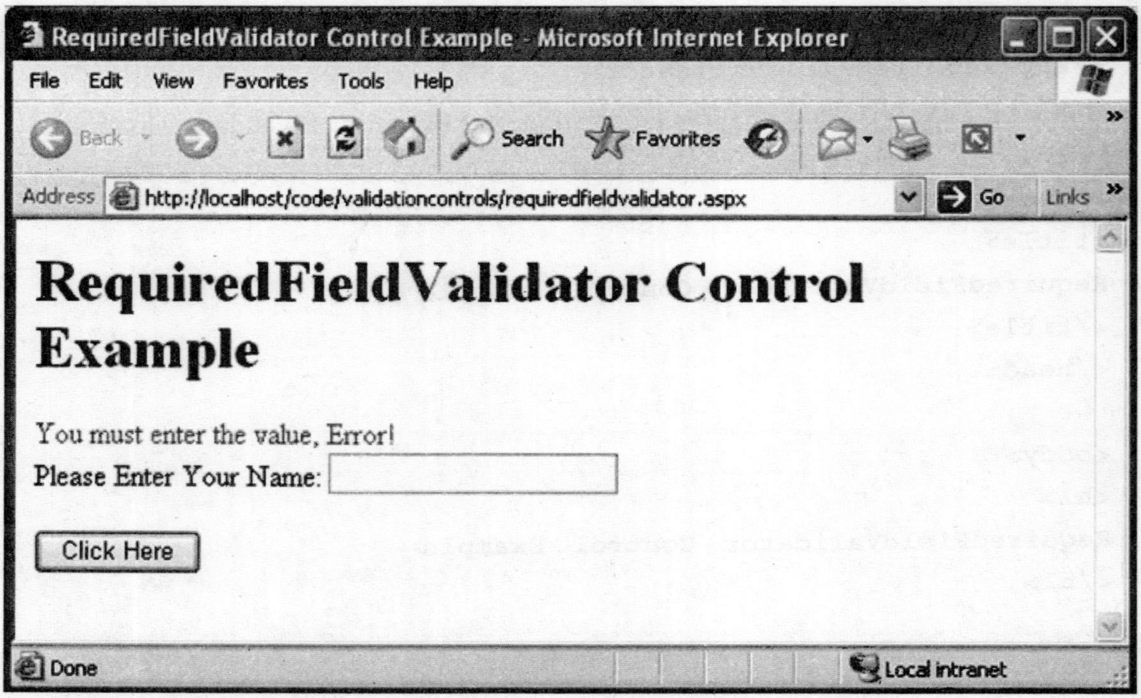

RANGEVALIDATOR CONTROL

This control validates the defined range. You can specify the minimum and maximum values criteria using MinimumValue and MaximumValue properties. To bind the control for range validation you can give the control name in ControlToValidate property.

The following code will demonstrate the implementation of RangeValidator Control:

```
<html>
<head>
<title>
RangeValidator Control Example
</title>
<script language="VB" runat="server">

Sub run_proc(sender As Object, e As EventArgs)

  RangeValidatorcontrol1.Validate()

  If (RangeValidatorcontrol1.IsValid) Then
  showtext.Text = "You have entered in between 5-50"
else
showtext.Text = "You have not entered in between 5-50"
 End If

End Sub
</script>
</head>

<body>
<h1>
RangeValidator Control Example
</h1>

<form runat=server>

<asp:TextBox Selected id="Textboxcontrol1" runat="server"/>
<br>
<br>
<asp:Label id="showtext" runat="server" />
```

```
<asp:RangeValidator      id="RangeValidatorcontrol1"
Type="Integer"   ControlToValidate="Textboxcontrol1"
MinimumValue="5" MaximumValue="50"   runat="server"/>
<br>
<br>
<asp:Button Text="Click Here" onclick="run_proc" runat="server"
/>
</form>

</body>
</html>
```

Output of the above code would be like this:

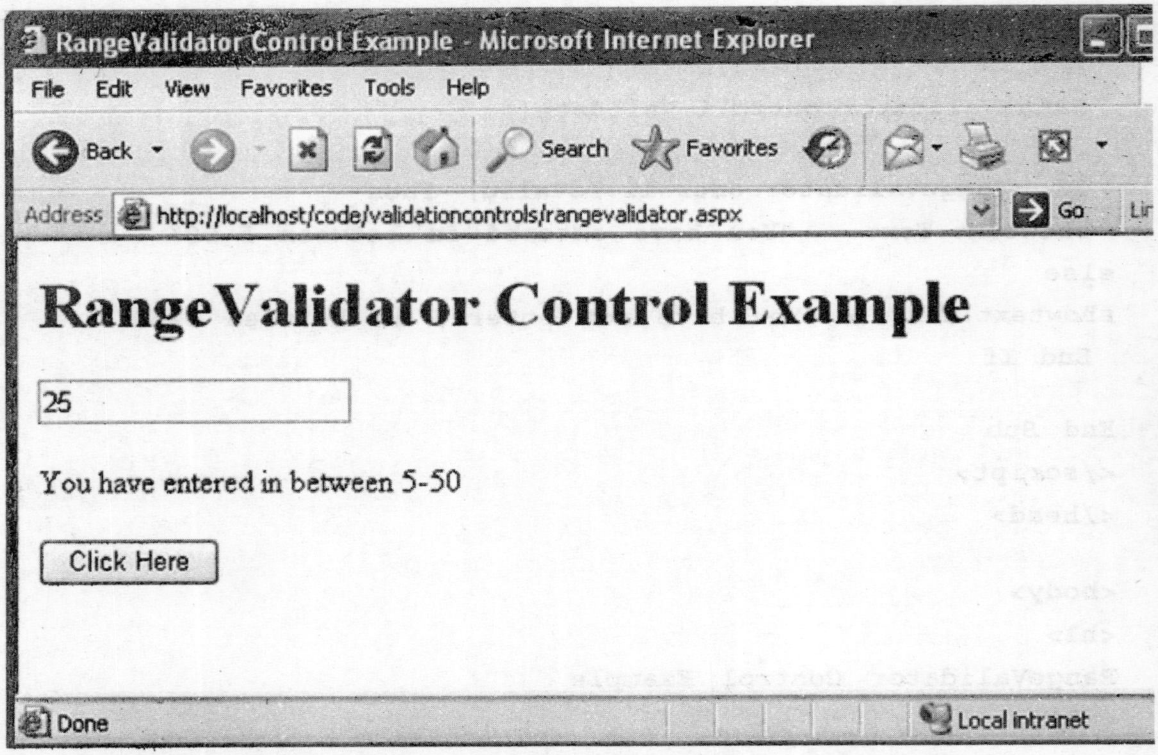

REGULAREXPRESSIONVALIDATOR CONTROL

The major role of Regularexpressionvalidator control is to confirm that the entry shouldmatches a pattern. This pattern is defined by a regular expression. Like this you can check the conditions or predictable sequences of characters like e-mail address, postal codes etc.

The following code will demonstrate the implementation of RegularExpressionValidator control:

```
<html>
<head>
<title>
RegularExpressionValidator Control Example
</title>
<script language="VB" runat="server">

        Sub run_proc(sender As Object, e As EventArgs)

           If Page.IsValid Then
              showtext.Text = "Page contains no Errors!"
           Else
              showtext.Text = "Page contains Errors!"
           End If

        End Sub

   </script>

</head>

<body>
<h1>
RegularExpressionValidator Control Example
</h1>

<form runat=server>

<br>
<br>
<ASP:Label id="showtext" runat="server" />
<br>
<br>
```

```
<ASP:TextBox id=TextBoxControl1 runat=server />

<asp:RegularExpressionValidator
id="RegularExpressionValidatorControl1" runat="server"
                    ControlToValidate="TextBoxControl1"
                         ValidationExpression="^[\w-]+@[\w-
]+\.(com|net)$"
                    Display="Static"
                 >
                         Error! E-mail address is not valid.
               </asp:RegularExpressionValidator>
<br>
<br>
<asp:requiredfieldvalidator id="requiredfieldvalidatorcontrol1"
controltovalidate="textboxcontrol1" runat=server
display="dynamic">Please enter E-mail address, Error!</
asp:requiredfieldvalidator>
<br>
<br>
<ASP:Button text="Click Here" OnClick="run_proc" runat=server
/>

</form>

</body>
</html>
```

Output of the RegularExpressionValidator control would be like the one shown on next page.

COMPAREVALIDATOR CONTROL

The basic purpose of Comparevalidator control is to compare the value of one control to another. It controls the explicit value in control's Valuetocompare property.

The following code will show the implementation of comparevalidator control:

```
<%@ Page clienttarget=downlevel %>

<html>
```

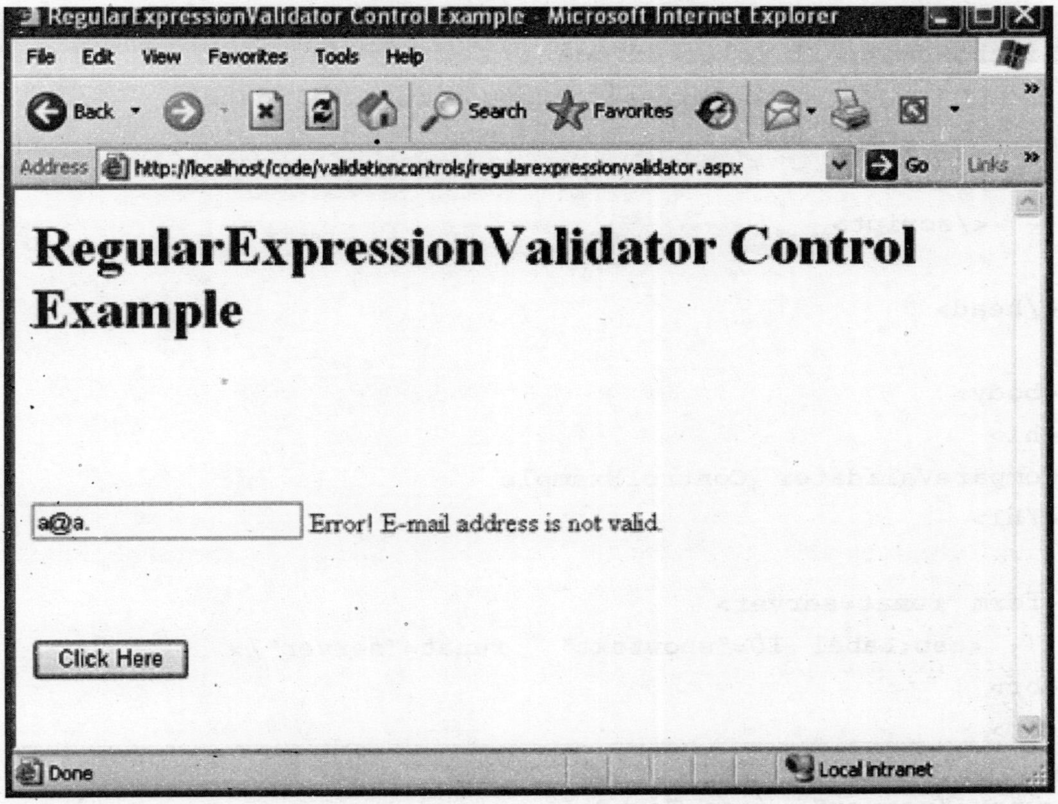


```
<head>
<title>
CompareValidator ControlExample
</title>
<script language="VB" runat="server">

        Sub run_proc(sender As Object, e As EventArgs)
            If Page.IsValid Then
              showtext.Text = "Page contains no Errors"
            Else
             showtext.Text = "Page contains Errors"
            End If
        End Sub

         Sub Listboxcontrol1_SelectedIndexChanged(sender As
Object, e As EventArgs)
```

```
                comparevalidatorcontrol1.Operator =
Listboxcontrol1.SelectedIndex
            comparevalidatorcontrol1.Validate
        End Sub

    </script>

</head>

<body>
<h1>
CompareValidator ControlExample
</h1>

<form runat=server>
    <asp:Label ID="showtext"  runat="server"/>
<br>
<Br>
<asp:TextBox Selected="True" id="Textboxcontrol1"
runat="server"></asp:TextBox>
<br>
<br>
<asp:ListBox                          id="Listboxcontrol1"
OnSelectedIndexChanged="Listboxcontrol1_SelectedIndexChanged"
runat="server">
  <asp:ListItem Value="GreaterThan" >GreaterThan</asp:ListItem>
<asp:ListItem Selected="True" Value="Equal" >Equal</
asp:ListItem>
  <asp:ListItem Value="NotEqual" >NotEqual</asp:ListItem>
<asp:ListItem Value="LessThan" >LessThan</asp:ListItem>
</asp:ListBox>
<Br>
<br>
  <asp:TextBox id="Textboxcontrol2" runat="server"></
asp:TextBox><p>
<br>
```

```
<br>
<asp:Button runat=server Text="Click here to compare"
onclick="run_proc" />
<asp:CompareValidator id="comparevalidatorcontrol1"
ControlToValidate="Textboxcontrol1" ControlToCompare =
"Textboxcontrol2" Type="String" runat="server"/>

</form>

</body>
</html>
```

Output would be like this:

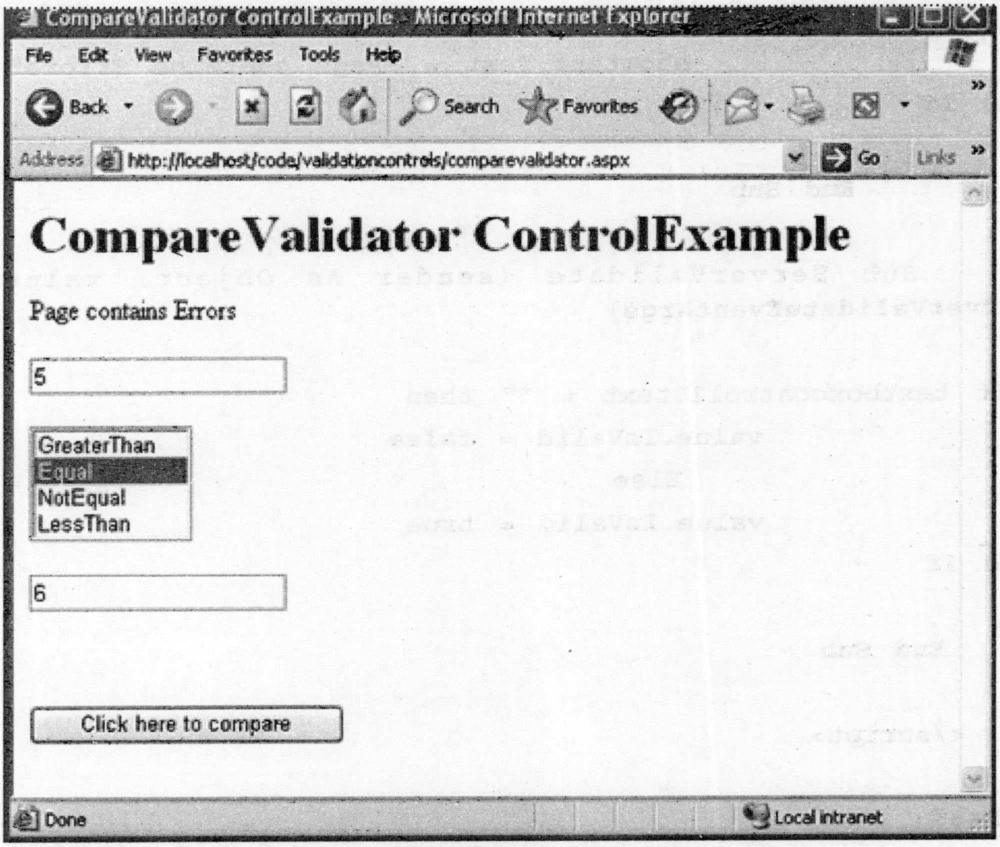

CUSTOMVALIDATOR CONTROL

For validation purpose this control calls a user-defined function. This custom function can be executed on the client-side script like VBScript or on the server side.

The following code will show the implementation of control:

```
<html>
<head>
<title>
CustomValidator  Control  Example
</title>
<script  language="VB"  runat=server>

          Sub  run_proc(sender  As  Object,  e  As  EventArgs)

If  (Page.IsValid)  Then
                    showtext.Text  =  "Page  contains  no  Errors"
               Else
                    showtext.Text  =  "Page  contains  Errors"
End  If

          End  Sub

      Sub  ServerValidate  (sender  As  Object,  value  As
ServerValidateEventArgs)

  If  textboxcontrol1.text  =  ""  then
               value.IsValid  =  false
                    Else
               value.IsValid  =  true
End  If

     End  Sub

    </script>

</head>

<body>
<h1>
```

```
CustomValidator Control Example
</h1>

<form runat=server>
<asp:Label id=showtext runat="server"
          Text="Please enter something:"
        />
<br>
<br>

 <asp:TextBox id=Textboxcontrol1 runat="server" />
<asp:CustomValidator id="Customvalidatorcontrol1" runat="server"
          ControlToValidate="Textboxcontrol1"
          OnServerValidate="ServerValidate"
          Display="Static"
          >
              Entered nothing!
      </asp:CustomValidator>


<br>
<br>

      <asp:Button text="Click here" onclick="run_proc"
runat="server" />

</form>

</body>
</html>
```

Output would be like the one shown on the next page.

VALIDATIONSUMMARY CONTROL

If your page contains any error then you can show that using ValidationSummary control. When all validation controls processed then according to user inputs IsValid property sets.

The following code will show the implementation of control:

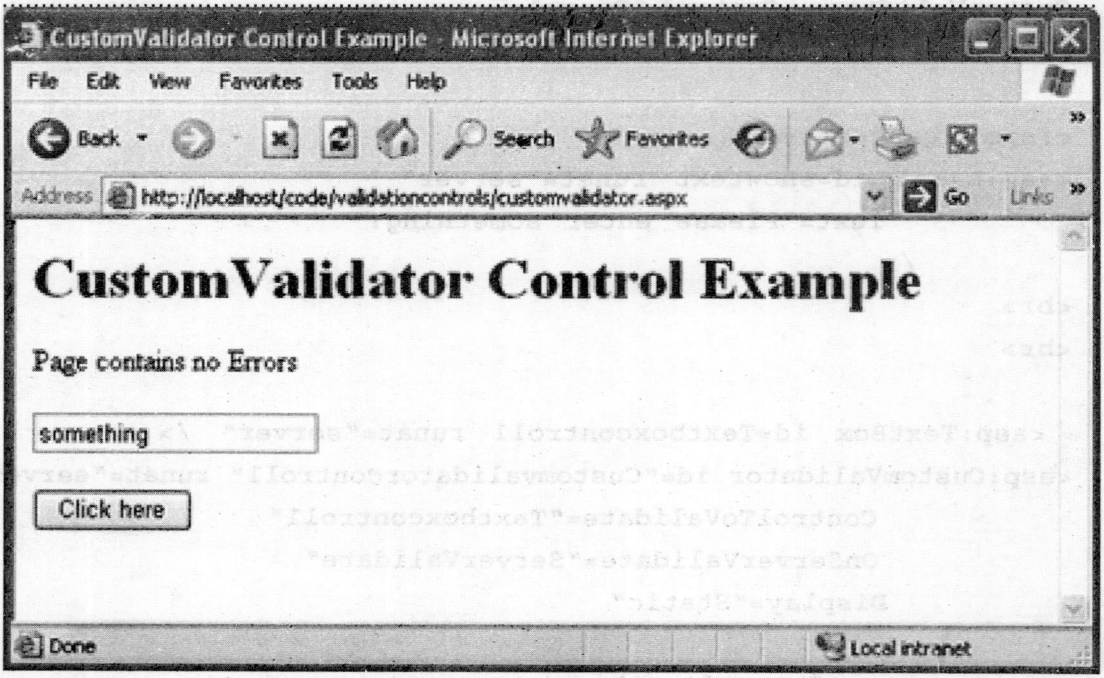


```
<html>
<head>
<title>
ValidationSummary Control Example
</title>
</head>

<body>
<h1>
ValidationSummary Control Example
</h1>

<form runat=server>

<asp:RequiredFieldValidator id="RequiredFieldValidator1"
ControlToValidate="Textboxcontrol1"   runat="server">
 You must enter the value, Error!
</asp:RequiredFieldValidator>
<br>
```

```
Please Enter Your Name: <asp:TextBox id=Textboxcontrol1
runat="server"/>
<br>
<br>
<asp:RequiredFieldValidator id="RequiredFieldValidator2"
ControlToValidate="Textboxcontrol2" runat="server">
 You must enter the value, Error!
</asp:RequiredFieldValidator>
<br>
Please Enter Your Name: <asp:TextBox id=Textboxcontrol2
runat="server"/>
<br>
<br>
<asp:Button Text="Click Here" runat="Server"
onserverclick="run_proc" />
<br>
<br>
<asp:ValidationSummary ID="validationcontrol1" runat="server"
                 HeaderText="Page Contains Errors! Please
check it out"
  />

</form>

</body>
</html>
```

Output would be like the one shown on the next page.

LOGIN CONTROL

Every dynamic site provides the functionally to a user to log into their web site and Login control provides such interface. For user authentication Login control uses the Membership service in your membership system.

The following code will show the implementation of control:

```
<html>
<head>
<title>
```

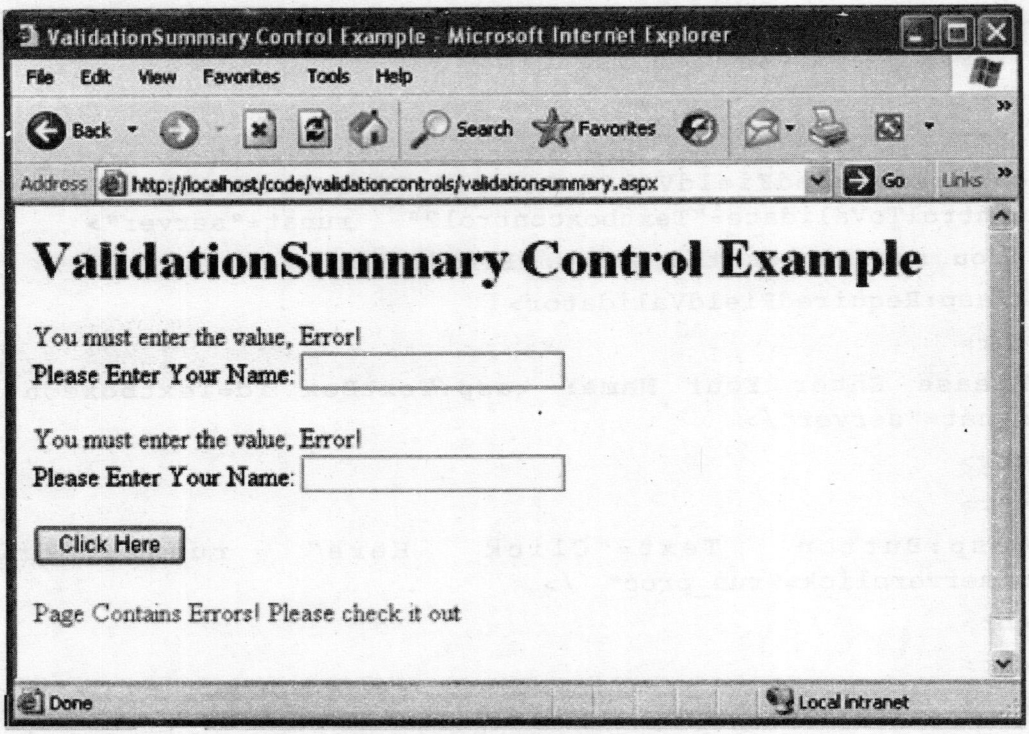


```
Login Control Example
</title>
</head>

<body>
<h1>
Login Control Example
</h1>

<form runat=server>

<asp:Login     ID="Logincontrol1"     runat="server"
BorderStyle="Solid" BorderWidth="2px"
DestinationPageUrl="makelogin.aspx" >
<TitleTextStyle   Font-Bold="True"   />
<InstructionTextStyle Font-Italic="True" ForeColor="Black" />
<LoginButtonStyle         BorderStyle="Solid" BorderWidth="2px"
/>
```

```
</asp:Login>

</form>

</body>
</html>
```

Output would be like this:

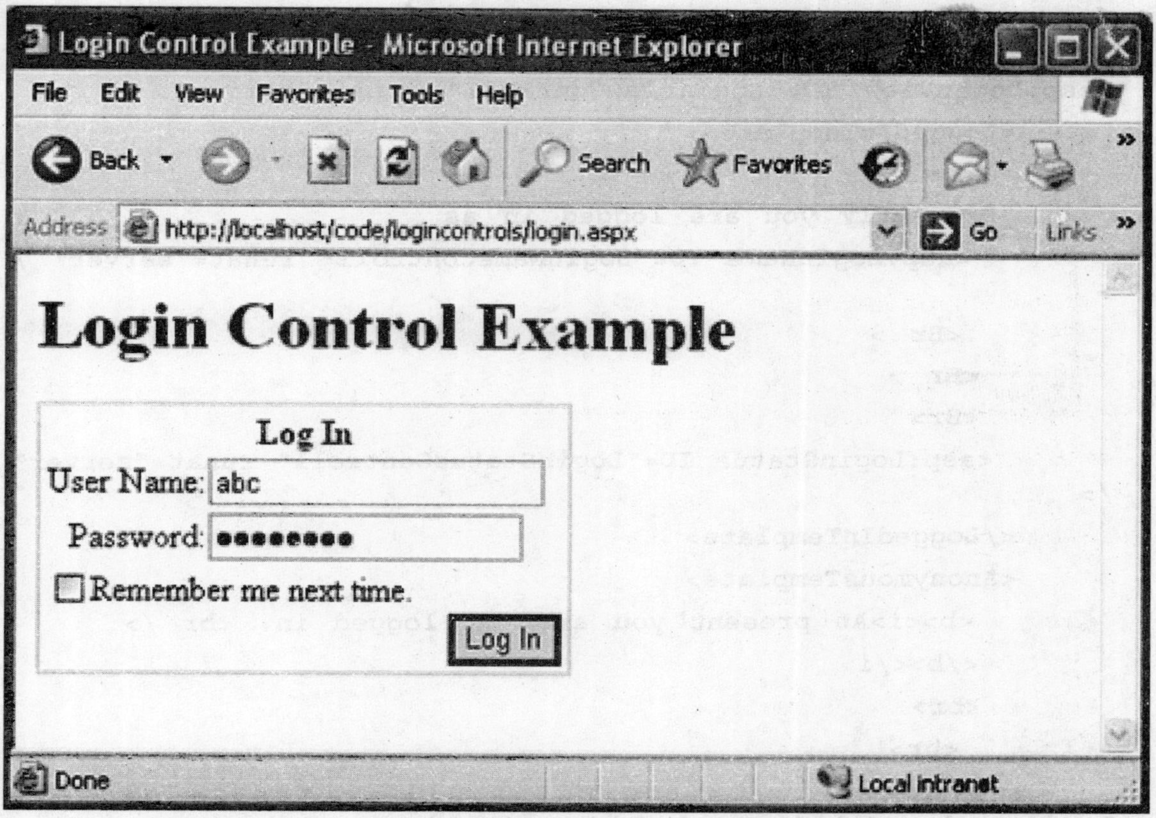

LOGINVIEW CONTROL

It automatically detects the user authentication status. It also detects the role of user.

The folowing code will show the implementation of control:

```
<html>
<head>
<title>
LoginView  Control  Example
```

```
</title>
</head>

<body>
<h1>
LoginView Control Example
</h1>

<form runat=server>
<asp:LoginView ID="LoginViewControl1" runat="server">
      <LoggedInTemplate>
        <br />
        Presently you are logged in as
         <asp:LoginName ID="LoginNameControl1" runat="server" /
>
        .<Br >
        <Br >
        <Br>
       <asp:LoginStatus ID="LoginStatusControl1" runat="server"
/>
      </LoggedInTemplate>
      <AnonymousTemplate>
         <b><i>At present you are not logged in. <br />
        </b></i>
        <br>
          <br>
   <asp:Login ID="LoginControl1" runat="server"
BorderStyle="Solid" BorderWidth="2px"
DestinationPageUrl="makelogin.aspx" >
<TitleTextStyle Font-Bold="True" />
<InstructionTextStyle Font-Italic="True" ForeColor="Black" />
<LoginButtonStyle        BorderStyle="Solid" BorderWidth="2px"
/>
  </asp:Login>
</AnonymousTemplate>
```

```
    </asp:LoginView>

  </form>

  </body>
  </html>
```

Output would be like this:

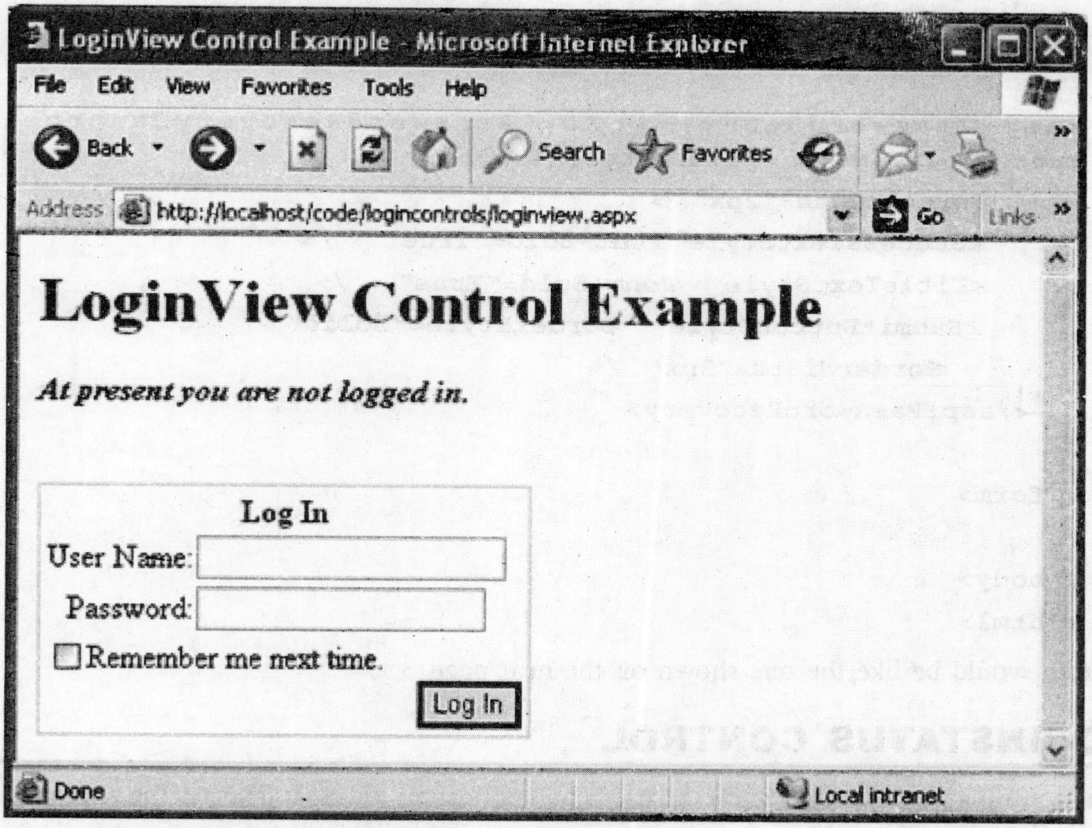

PASSWORDRECOVERY CONTROL

Using this control you can give the functionality to user to reset or retrieve user's password.

The following code will show the implementation of control:

```
<html>
<head>
<title>
PasswordRecovery  Control  Example
```

```
</title>
</head>

<body>
<h1>
PasswordRecovery  Control  Example
</h1>

<form  runat=server>

<asp:PasswordRecovery  ID="PasswordRecoveryControl1"
runat="server"     BorderStyle="Solid"
     BorderWidth="2px"  >
      <SuccessTextStyle Font-Bold="True"    />
      <TitleTextStyle   Font-Bold="True"    />
      <SubmitButtonStyle   BorderStyle="Solid"
         BorderWidth="2px"  />
   </asp:PasswordRecovery>

</form>

</body>
</html>
```

Output would be like the one shown on the next page.

LOGINSTATUS CONTROL

This control automatically detects the user's authentication status. It displays the appropriate Login/Logout option.

The following code will show the implementation of control:

```
<html>
<head>
<title>
LoginStatus  Control  Example
</title>
</head>
```

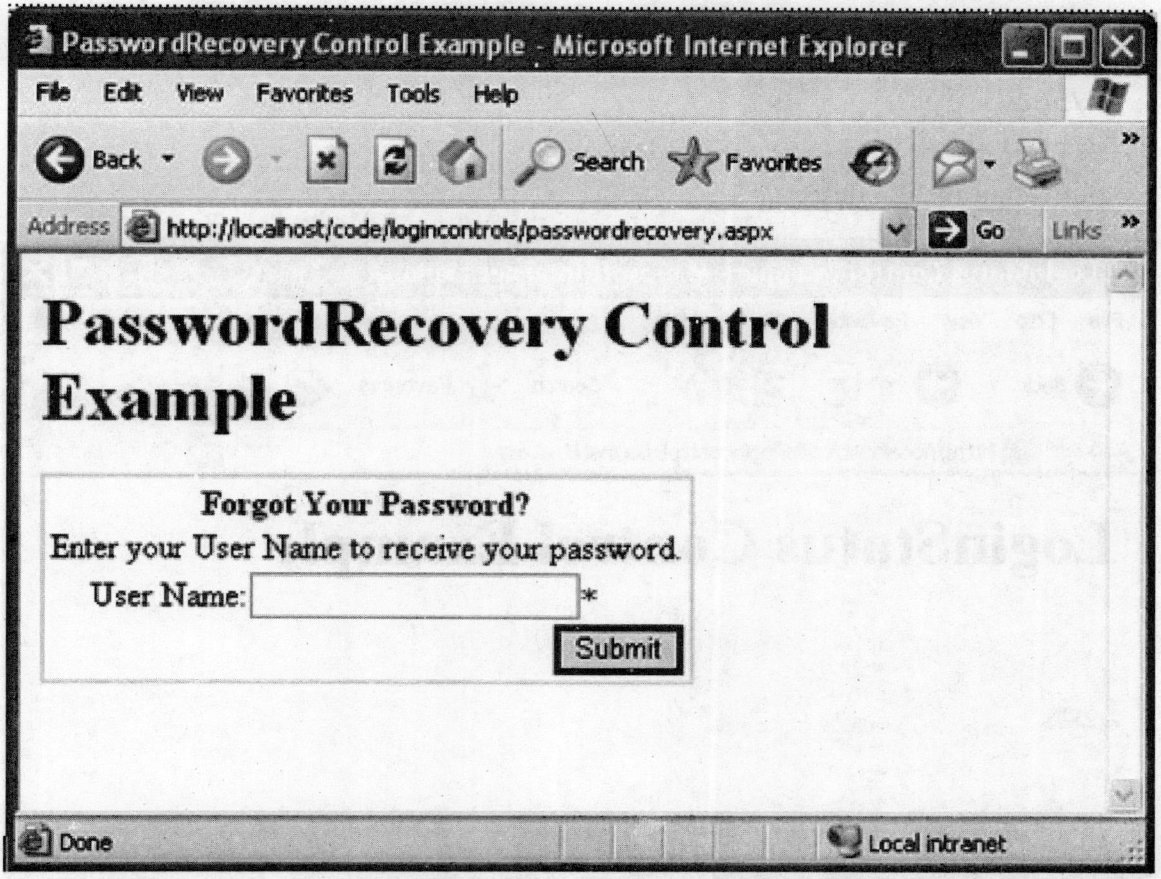


```
<body>
<h1>
LoginStatus Control Example
</h1>

<form runat=server>

  <asp:LoginName ID="Login1"  FormatString="Welcome {0}!"
runat="server" />
      <br >
      <br>
         <asp:LoginStatus ID="LoginStatuscontrol1"
runat="server"/>
```

```
</form>

</body>
</html>
```

Output would be like this:

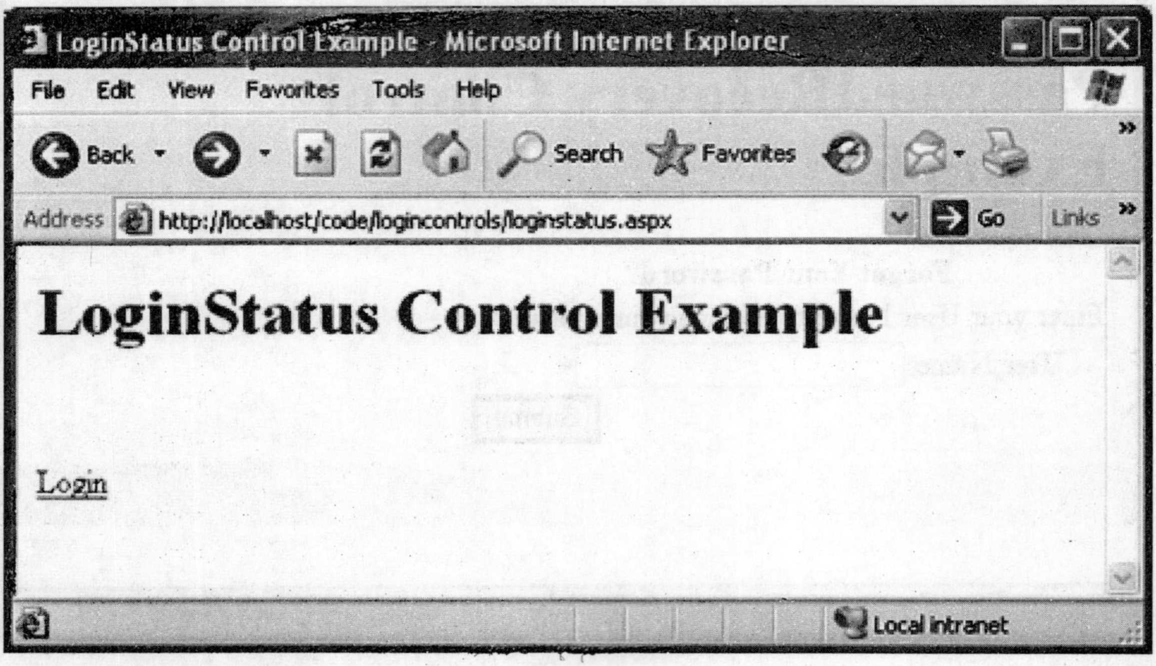

LOGINNAME CONTROL

This control displays the currently authenticated user's name on the page.

The following code will show the implementation of control:

```
<html>
<head>
<title>
LoginName Control Example
</title>
</head>

<body>
<h1>
LoginName Control Example
```

```
</h1>

<form runat=server>

<asp:LoginName ID="LoginNameControl1" FormatString="Welcome
{0}!" runat="server" />

<br>
 <br>
<asp:LoginStatus ID="LoginStatusControl1" runat="server"/>

</form>

</body>
</html>
```

Output would be like this:

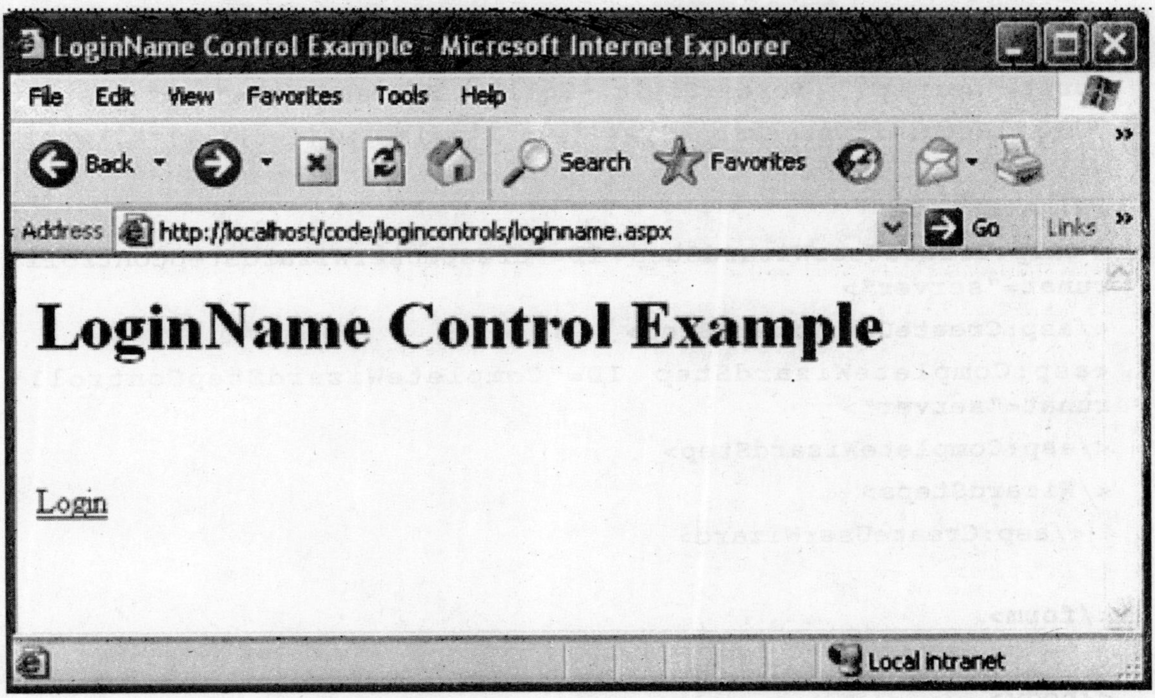

CREATEUSERWIZARD CONTROL

Using this control you can add the functionality in your Web site for creating new user.

The following code will show the implementation of control:

```
<html>
<head>
<title>
CreateUserWizard Control Example
</title>
</head>

<body>
<h1>
CreateUserWizard Control Example
</h1>

<form runat=server>

<asp:CreateUserWizard ID="CreateUserWizardControl1"
runat="server"  BorderStyle="Solid" BorderWidth="1px"
 EmailRegularExpression="\w+([-+.']\w+)*@\w+([-.]\w+)*\.\w+([-
.]\w+)*">
<WizardSteps>
 <asp:CreateUserWizardStep ID="CreateUserWizardStepControl1"
runat="server">
</asp:CreateUserWizardStep>
<asp:CompleteWizardStep ID="CompleteWizardStepControl1"
runat="server">
</asp:CompleteWizardStep>
</WizardSteps>
 </asp:CreateUserWizard>

</form>

</body>
</html>
```

Output would be like the one shown on the next page.

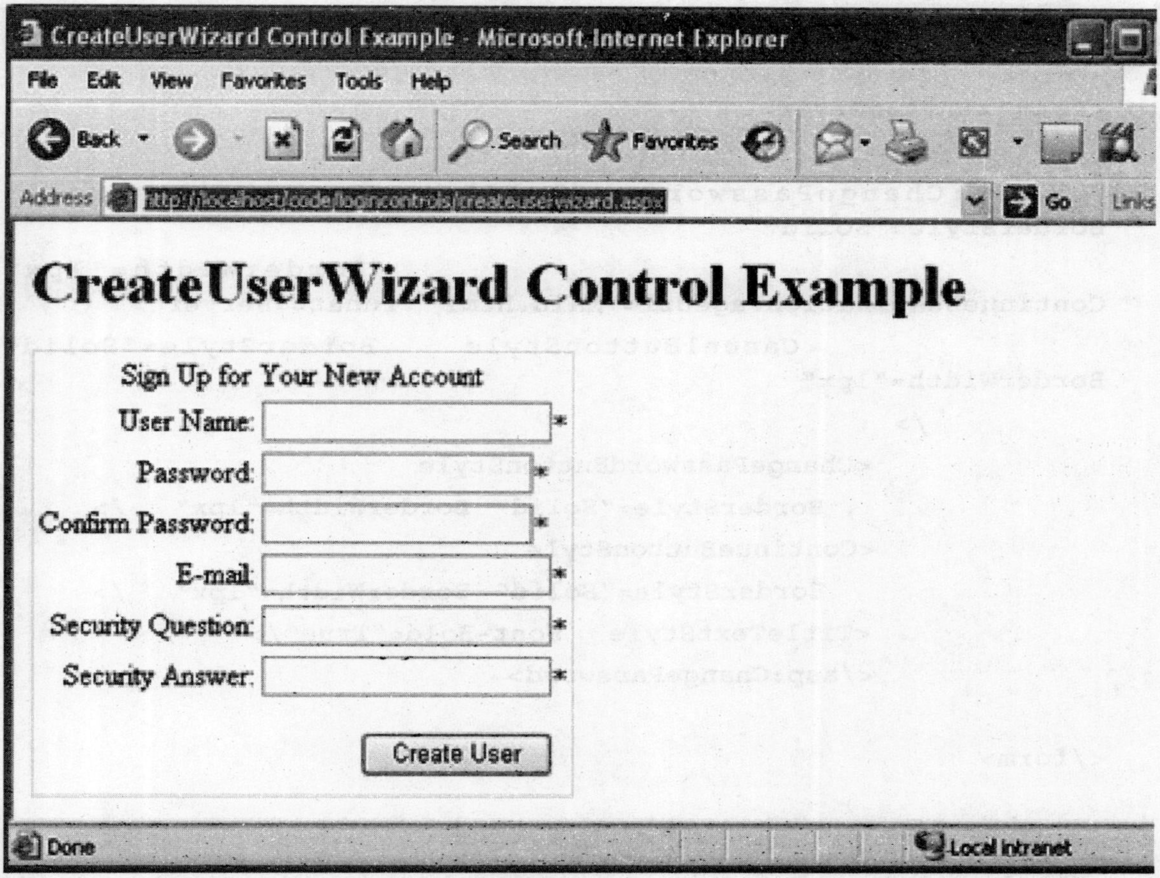

CHANGEPASSWORD CONTROL

Using this control you can give the functionality to user to change their password.

The following code will show the implementation of control:

```
<html>
<head>
<title>
ChangePassword Control Example
</title>
</head>

<body>
<h1>
ChangePassword Control Example
```

```
</h1>

<form runat=server>

   <asp:ChangePassword ID="ChangePasswordControl1"
BorderStyle="Solid"
                                          BorderWidth="1px"
ContinueDestinationPageUrl="Main.html" runat="server">
          <CancelButtonStyle BorderStyle="Solid"
BorderWidth="1px"
      />
        <ChangePasswordButtonStyle
          BorderStyle="Solid" BorderWidth="1px" />
        <ContinueButtonStyle
          BorderStyle="Solid" BorderWidth="1px" />
        <TitleTextStyle Font-Bold="True"/>
        </asp:ChangePassword>

</form>

</body>
</html>
```

Output would be like the one shown on the next page.

USER CONTROLS

User Controls are useful when you want to create your own control which works on your own logic. Basically this is your control and not available in built-in ASP.Net Web Server controls. In User control you can include markup and Web server controls. You can also define properties and methods to increase the functionality of your own control.

Once the control is created then you can reuse them as many times you want. Once the control is developed then you can add it to ASP.Net Web page like you add other controls.

On the time of creating User control you have an option to include it in separate page with extension .aspx. Generally when you keep the User control in a separate file its extension is recognized as .aspx. User control contains @ Control directive which covers configuration, properties etc. User control does not contain body, html, form elements. All such elements reside in a hosting page. Although you can use other HTML elements and Web controls on a User control.

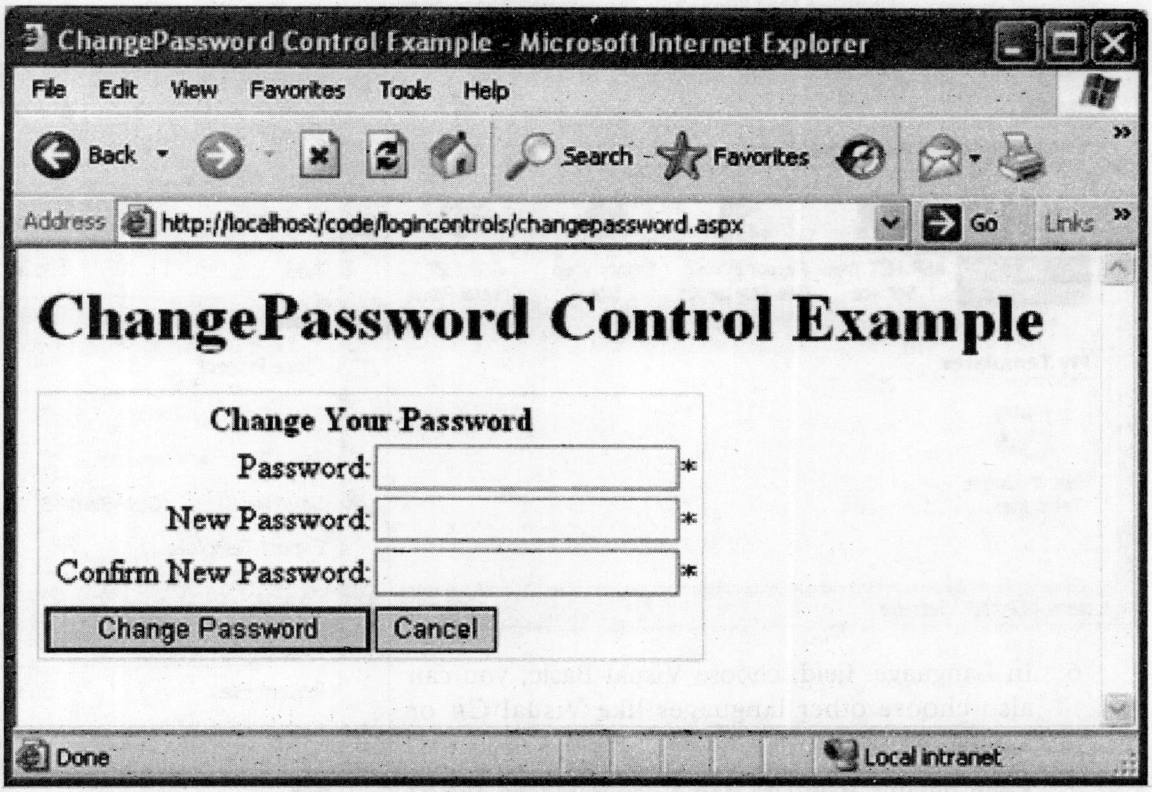

Once the User control is developed then you can add it to a Web page by registering it on the host page. You have to tell .ascx file which includes the User control, tag name and a tag prefix which are used for declaration of User control on the page.

You can also handle events in User control. For this you have to write a code in the User control to handle the events raised by the child controls but by default events raised by child controls are not available to the host page. Once you define the event then you can raise it.

CREATING USER CONTROL

To create a new User control, let we first create a new Web site in Visual Studio 2005. We are going to create such User control which will display the date.

1. Click on the File menu.
2. Click New Web Site…
3. New Web Site dialog box appears:
4. Under Templates: select ASP.NET Web Site.
5. In Location: field, choose File System.

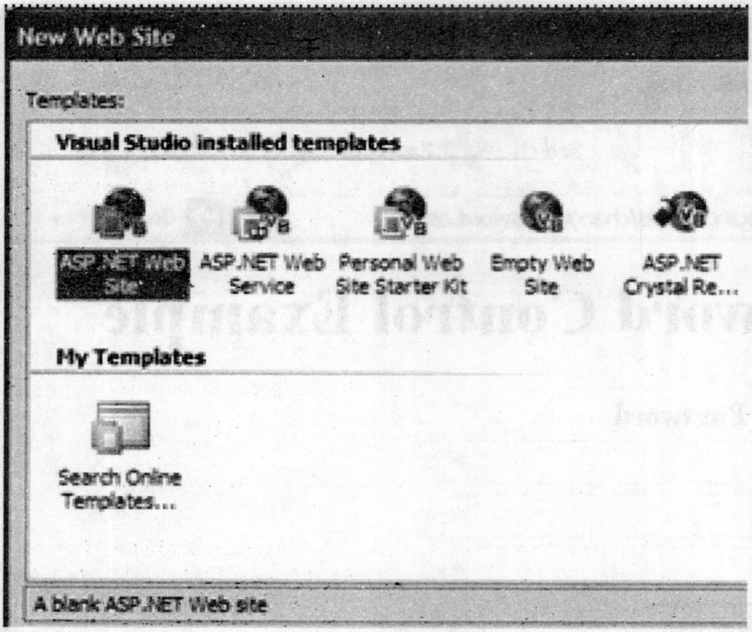

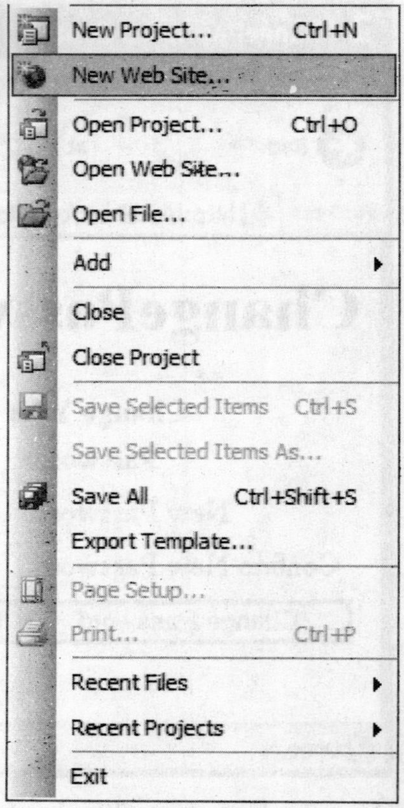

6. In Language: field, choose Visual Basic, you can also choose other languages like Visual C# or Visual J#.
7. Keep default Web site name generated by Visual Studio. To specify different location and name click on Browse button.
8. Click on OK button.
9. In Solution Explorer, right-click on Project name.
10. Click on Add New Item.
11. Add New Item dialog box appears.
12. Under Templates select Web User Control.
13. In Name field, type myfirstWebUserControl.ascx.
14. In Language field, select Visual Basic or select the desired language which is familiar to you for coding purpose.
15. Select the Place code in separate file option, this will keep all User control code in a separate file.
16. Click on Add button.
17. Notice the Solution Explorer window, myfirstWebUserControl.ascx file has been added.

Note: Default.aspx is your Web page and you will add the myfirstWebUserControl to this Web page or any other Web page. Now whatever logic you will implement on myfirstWebUserControl User control. You can use this control as many times you want.

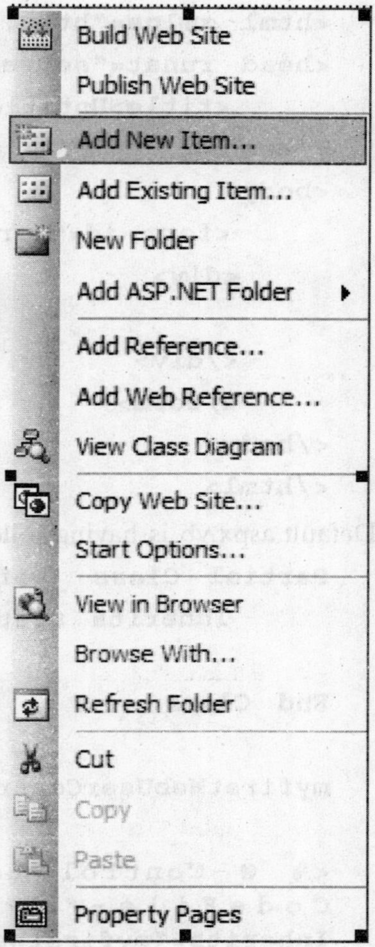

Let we run through all files individually the kind of code they contain at present.

Web page is having following code:

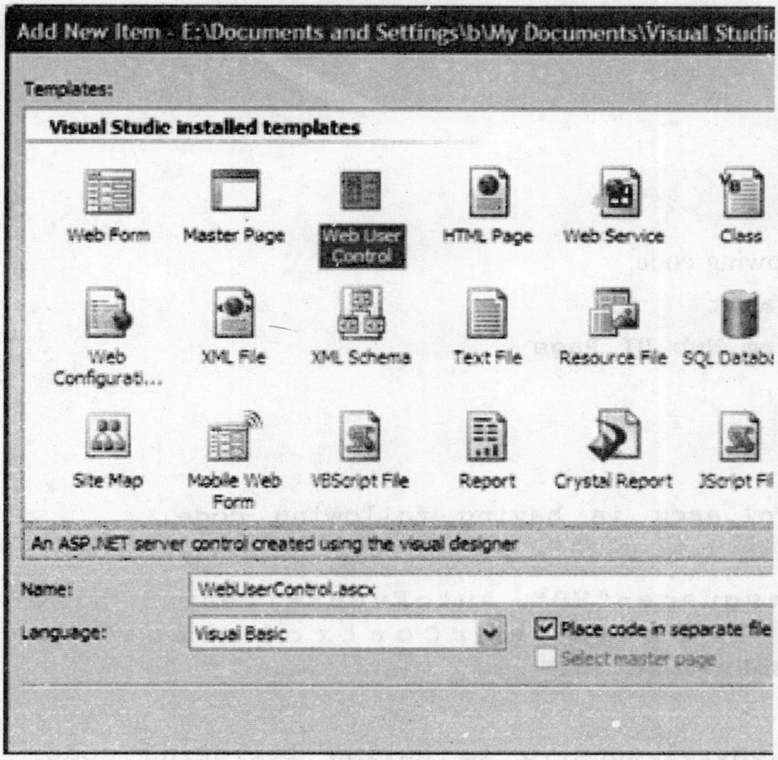


```
<%@    Page    Language="VB"
AutoEventWireup="false"
CodeFile="Default.aspx.vb"
Inherits="_Default" %>

<!DOCTYPE html PUBLIC "-//W3C//DTD
XHTML 1.0 Transitional//EN" "http://
www.w3.org/TR/xhtml1/DTD/xhtml1-
transitional.dtd">
```

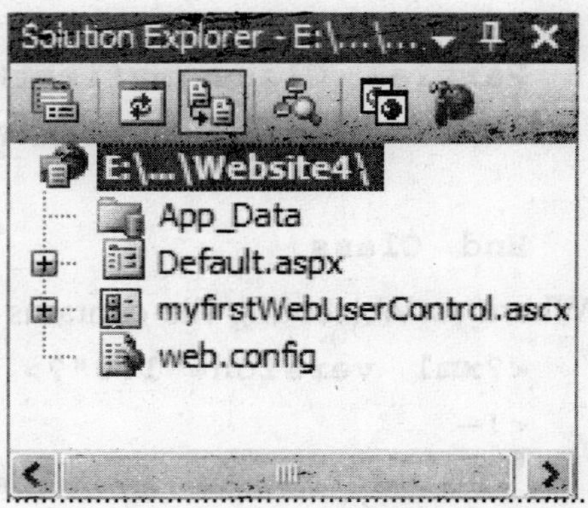

```
<html xmlns="http://www.w3.org/1999/xhtml" >
<head runat="server">
    <title>Untitled Page</title>
</head>
<body>
    <form id="form1" runat="server">
    <div>

    </div>
    </form>
</body>
</html>
```

Default.aspx.vb is having following code:

```
Partial Class _Default
    Inherits System.Web.UI.Page

End Class
```

myfirstWebUserControl.ascx is having following code:

```
<% @ Control Language="VB" AutoEventWireup="false"
CodeFile="myfirstWebUserControl.ascx.vb"
Inherits="myfirstWebUserControl" %>
```

And myfirstWebUserControl.ascx.vb is having following code:

```
Partial Class myfirstWebUserControl
    Inherits System.Web.UI.UserControl

End Class
```

Where as Web.config file contains the following code:

```
<?xml version="1.0"?>
<!–
    Note: As an alternative to hand editing this file you
can use the
```

```
    web admin tool to configure settings for your application.
Use
    the Website->Asp.Net Configuration option in Visual Studio.
    A full list of settings and comments can be found in
    machine.config.comments usually located in
    \Windows\Microsoft.Net\Framework\v2.x\Config
-->
<configuration>
    <appSettings/>
    <connectionStrings/>
    <system.web>
        <!--
            Set compilation debug="true" to insert debugging
              symbols into the compiled page. Because this
            affects performance, set this value to true only
              during development.

              Visual Basic options:
                Set strict="true" to disallow all data type
conversions
              where data loss can occur.
              Set explicit="true" to force declaration of all
variables.
        -->
            <compilation debug="false" strict="false"
explicit="true" />
        <pages>
            <namespaces>
                <clear />
                <add namespace="System" />
                <add namespace="System.Collections" />
                                                      <add
namespace="System.Collections.Specialized" />
                <add namespace="System.Configuration" />
                <add namespace="System.Text" />
```

```
                                                    <add
  namespace="System.Text.RegularExpressions" />
                <add namespace="System.Web" />
                <add namespace="System.Web.Caching" />
                <add namespace="System.Web.SessionState" /
  >
                <add namespace="System.Web.Security" />
                <add namespace="System.Web.Profile"/>
                <add namespace="System.Web.UI" />
                <add namespace="System.Web.UI.WebControls"
  />
                                                    <add
  namespace="System.Web.UI.WebControls.WebParts" />
               <add namespace="System.Web.UI.HtmlControls"
  />
          </namespaces>
       </pages>
       <!-
               The <authentication> section enables
  configuration
          of the security authentication mode used by
          ASP.NET to identify an incoming user.
       ->
       <authentication mode="Windows" />
       <!-
          The <customErrors> section enables configuration
          of what to do if/when an unhandled error occurs
          during the execution of a request. Specifically,
           it enables developers to configure html error
  pages
          to be displayed in place of a error stack trace.

                <customErrors   mode="RemoteOnly"
  defaultRedirect="GenericErrorPage.htm">
          <error statusCode="403" redirect="NoAccess.htm"
  />
```

```
                                    <error statusCode="404"
redirect="FileNotFound.htm" />
            </customErrors>
            ->
        </system.web>
</configuration>
```

Now this is the right time to add some functionality to our User control.

18. Select the myfirstWebUserControl.ascx file.

19. Click the View Designer option in Solution Explorer window.

20. In Standard Toolbox double-click the Literal control to add it.

21. Set the Id of this literal control to mydisplaydate
22. Now double-click on myfirstWebUserControl.ascx.vb in Solution Explorer.
23. It will open the code window. Type the following code:

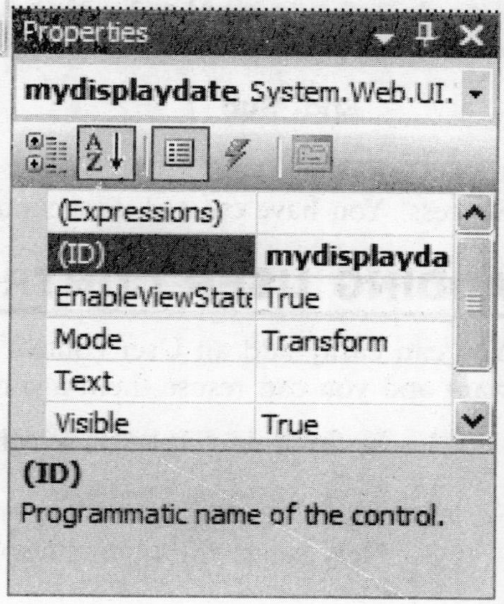


```
Protected Sub Page_Load(ByVal sender
As    Object,    ByVal    e    As
System.EventArgs) Handles Me.Load
```

```
mydisplaydate.Text = DateTime.Today.ToLongDateString

End Sub
```

24. Your final myfirstWebUserControl.ascx.vb code file should be like this:

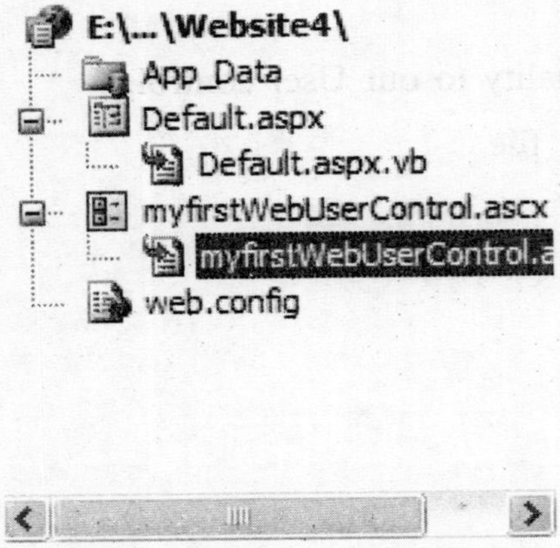


```
Partial Class myfirstWebUserControl
    Inherits System.Web.UI.UserControl

    Protected Sub Page_Load(ByVal sender As Object, ByVal e
As System.EventArgs) Handles Me.Load

        mydisplaydate.Text = DateTime.Today.ToLongDateString

    End Sub
End Class
```

Success! You have created user control which will display the date.

ADDING USER CONTROL

You can easily add an User control to any Web page in the same site as many times you want and you can resuse them again and again. For this perform the following steps:

1. In Solution Explorer, select the Default.aspx file
2. Click on View Designer
3. Now select the myfirstWebUserControl in Solution Explorer window.

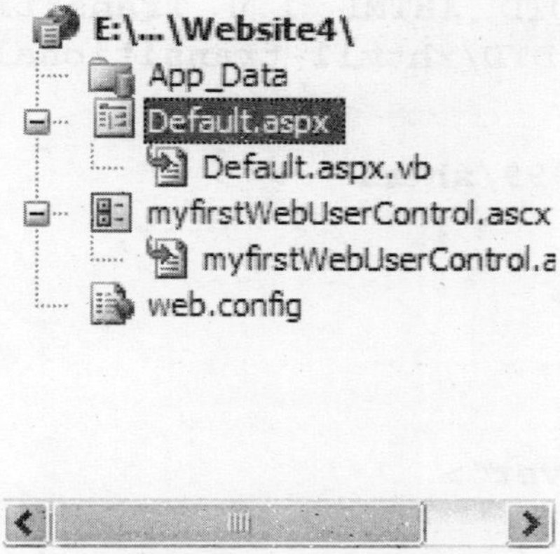

4. Drag and drop this control to Default.aspx Web page which is active at present, like this you can this your created User control to any Web page in same site.

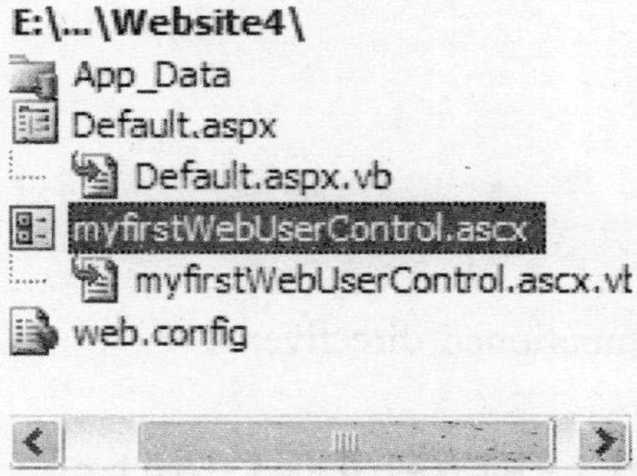

5. Notice on Web page that user control has been added.

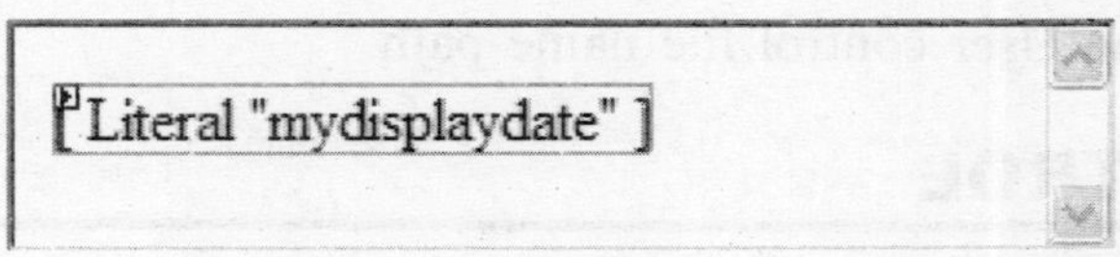

Once the control is added it is registered on the added page. Notice the code below of default.aspx page:

```
<%@ Page Language="VB" AutoEventWireup="false"
CodeFile="Default.aspx.vb" Inherits="_Default"%>


<%@ Register Src="myfirstWebUserControl.ascx"
TagName="myfirstWebUserControl" TagPrefix="uc1"%>
```

```
<!DOCTYPE html PUBLIC "-//W3C//DTD XHTML 1.0 Transitional//
EN" "http://www.w3.org/TR/xhtml1/DTD/xhtml1-transitional.dtd">

<html xmlns="http://www.w3.org/1999/xhtml" >
<head runat="server">
     <title>Untitled Page</title>
</head>
<body>
     <form id="form1" runat="server">
    <div>
         <uc1:myfirstWebUserControl ID="MyfirstWebUserControl1"
runat="server" />

    </div>
    </form>
</body>
</html>
```

In this page at top you can find the following mentioned directive:

```
<%@ Register Src="myfirstWebUserControl.ascx"
TagName="myfirstWebUserControl" TagPrefix="uc1"%>
```

Where as Src attribute contains the User control file name path.

TESTING USER CONTROL

1. To test and run, Click on Start button.
2. Debugging Not Enabled dialog box appears.
3. Select second option, Run without debugging. (Equivalent to Ctrl + F5).
4. Click on OK button.
5. The Web page is opened in a Web browser with User control added on it.
6. It is displaying the date.

Just notice the myfirstWebUserControl.ascx.vb file. We have written the following code in it:

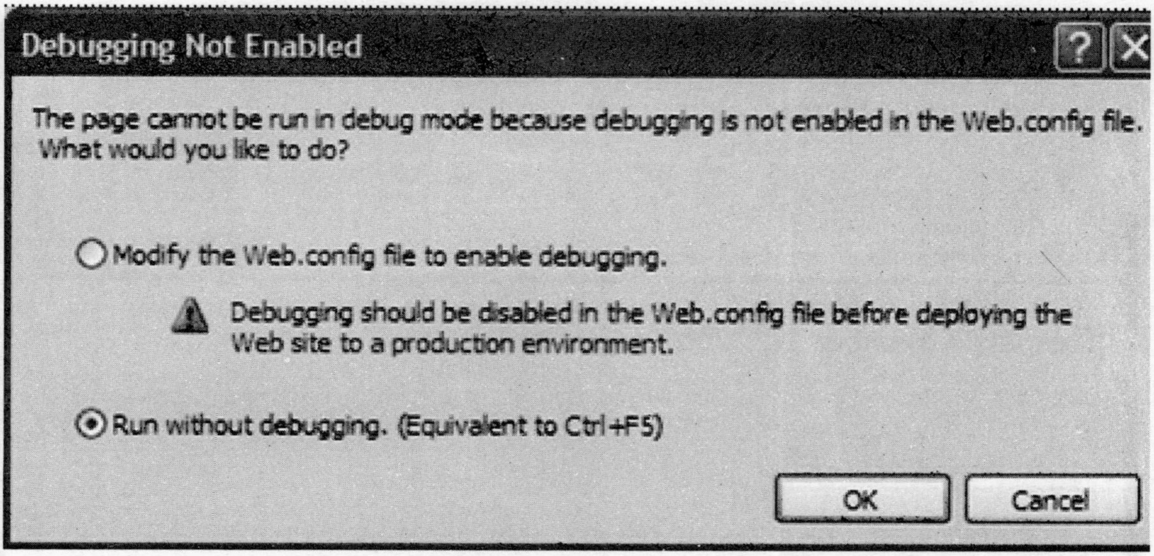


```
Partial Class myfirstWebUserControl
    Inherits System.Web.UI.UserControl
    Protected Sub Page_Load(ByVal sender As Object, ByVal e
As System.EventArgs) Handles Me.Load
        mydisplaydate.Text = DateTime.Today.ToLongDateString
    End Sub
End Class
```

Mydisplaydate is a literal control used here to display the data and we are storing Date through DateTime.Today.ToLongDateString command in the text property of literal control.

In any page if you add this control that page will display the date. Like this you can create any kind of User control according to your business or any other logic.

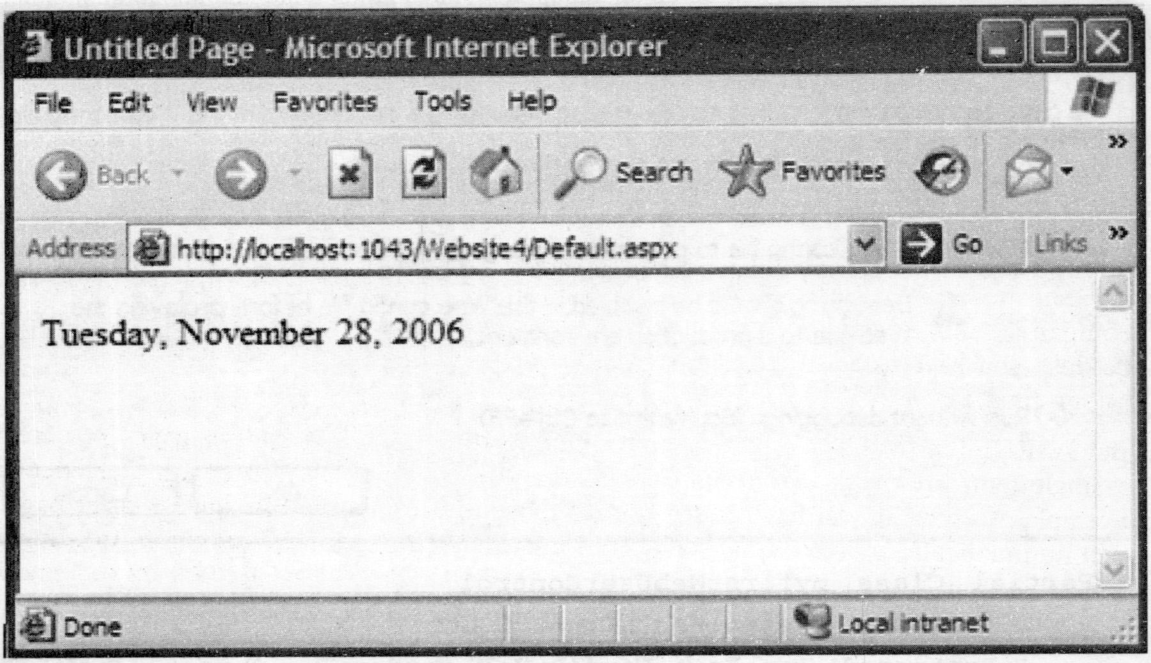
Untitled Page - Microsoft Internet Explorer
File Edit View Favorites Tools Help
Back
Search
Favorites
Address
http://localhost:1043/Website4/Default.aspx
Go
Links
Tuesday, November 28, 2006
Done
Local intranet

4 Master Pages and CSS

INTRODUCTION

Imagine your Web site contains several Web pages. You have uploaded them and they are working fine. Each Web site may contain 30 or 50 Web pages and after few days your company wants to add more pages for their new product. The task becomes complicated because you have to add the reference of this new URL to all 50 Web pages. It may take a long time.

But ASP.NET provides one ultimate technique for this, known as Master page. You create a single template on this page which is a common page for all Web pages. Consider the example of above if you have added the reference of all links in this single Master page it will automatically reflect on all Web pages and all Web pages have common links layout generated from this Master page. You have to then only design and fix text on this master page only. Images, which you want to show in particular pages, need to have links of other Web pages because they will be automatically generated from Master page.

Then you need to add link of this new Web page, which is being added, to Master page. Automatically all 50 Web pages will have a new added link through Master page and you do not need to fix the link individually to all 50 Web pages.

Master page is a build up of master page itself and one or more content pages.So through Master page you create a consistent layout. Look and feel for all Web pages belong to your Web site. Once the layout is defined in a Master page then you can create individual content pages of particular Web pages which you want to show. Whenever these content pages are requested from visitors, these pages are merged with the master page, which is a combination of the master page and content of content page of particular Web page.

The file extension of master page is .master. Master page can include HTML elements, server controls, text, etc. Master page is identified by @ Master directive.

For example:

```
<%@ Master Language="VB" %>
```

If you add a new Master page to your Web site you will find such code in a master page with master directive at top which is replaced with the @ page directive.

```
<%@ Master Language="VB" CodeFile="MasterPage.master.vb"
Inherits="MasterPage"%>
<!DOCTYPE html PUBLIC "-//W3C//DTD XHTML 1.0 Transitional//
```

```
EN" "http://www.w3.org/TR/xhtml1/DTD/xhtml1-transitional.dtd">

<html xmlns="http://www.w3.org/1999/xhtml" >
<head runat="server">
    <title>Untitled Page</title>
</head>
<body>
    <form id="form1" runat="server">
    <div>
            <asp:contentplaceholder id="ContentPlaceHolder1"
runat="server">
          </asp:contentplaceholder>
    </div>
    </form>
</body>
</html>
```

If you have selected Place code in separate file option then <name of master page> .master.vb file will contain the following code:

```
Partial Class MasterPage
    Inherits System.Web.UI.MasterPage
End Class
```

Now for the layout your master page can contain all top-level HTML elements like html, head, form etc. To add the company logo in all Web pages you can use img element in your master page. To add links or copyright information at bottom you may add text in master page.

Now you have to define some space in master page where you can add different type of information in different Web pages. For this you can have one or more Contentplaceholder controls in a Master page. These Contentplaceholder controls actually defines the regions where replaceable information or data will appear. These replaceable contents can be placed in different Web pages which are known as content pages in case if you add master page to your Web site.

Now after creating master page to your site when you will add the Web page or Web form in your Web site you have an option to generate that Web form with the combination of master page for common layout.

Basically you bound this Web form or Web page to a specific master page. You may notice this binding at the top of the .aspx file or your Web form file in @ Page directive.

For example:

```
<%@ Page Language="VB" MasterPageFile="~/MasterPage.master"
AutoEventWireup="false" CodeFile="Default.aspx.vb"
Inherits="_Default" title="Untitled Page"%>
```

Now your complete Web form will contain following code:

```
<%@ Page Language="VB" MasterPageFile="~/MasterPage.master"
AutoEventWireup="false" CodeFile="Default.aspx.vb"
Inherits="_Default" title="Untitled Page"%>
<asp:Content ID="Content1"
ContentPlaceHolderID="ContentPlaceHolder1" Runat="Server">
</asp:Content>
```

In content pages or your can say your Web forms you can add text or controls or code according to logic in these contentplaceholders.

Finally using Master pages you can update the things at one place which saves your time and headache both.

CREATING A WEB SITE WITH MASTER PAGE

For this let we first create a basic Web site using Visual Studio 2005. Perform the following steps first:

1. Click on the File menu.
2. Click New Web Site.
3. New Web Site dialog box appears:
4. Under Templates: select ASP.NET Web Site.
5. In Location: field, choose File System.
6. In Language: field, choose Visual Basic, you can also choose other languages like Visual C# or Visual J#.
7. Keep default Web site name generated by Visual Studio. To specify different location and name click on Browse button.
8. Click on OK button.

   At this time your Solution Explorer window may look like this:

   We have to delete the Default.aspx page because we will generate this through master page for common layout of our Web site.

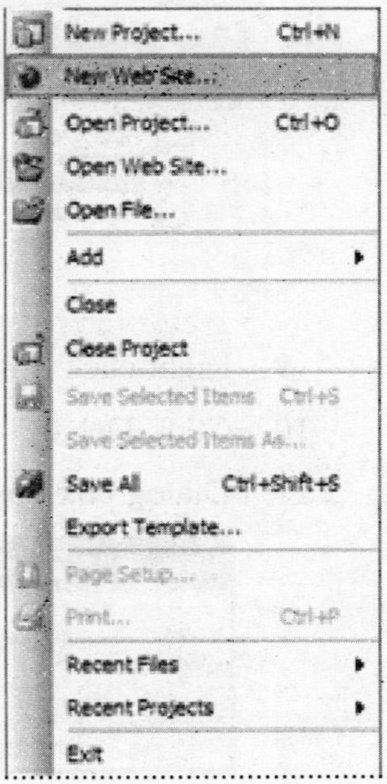

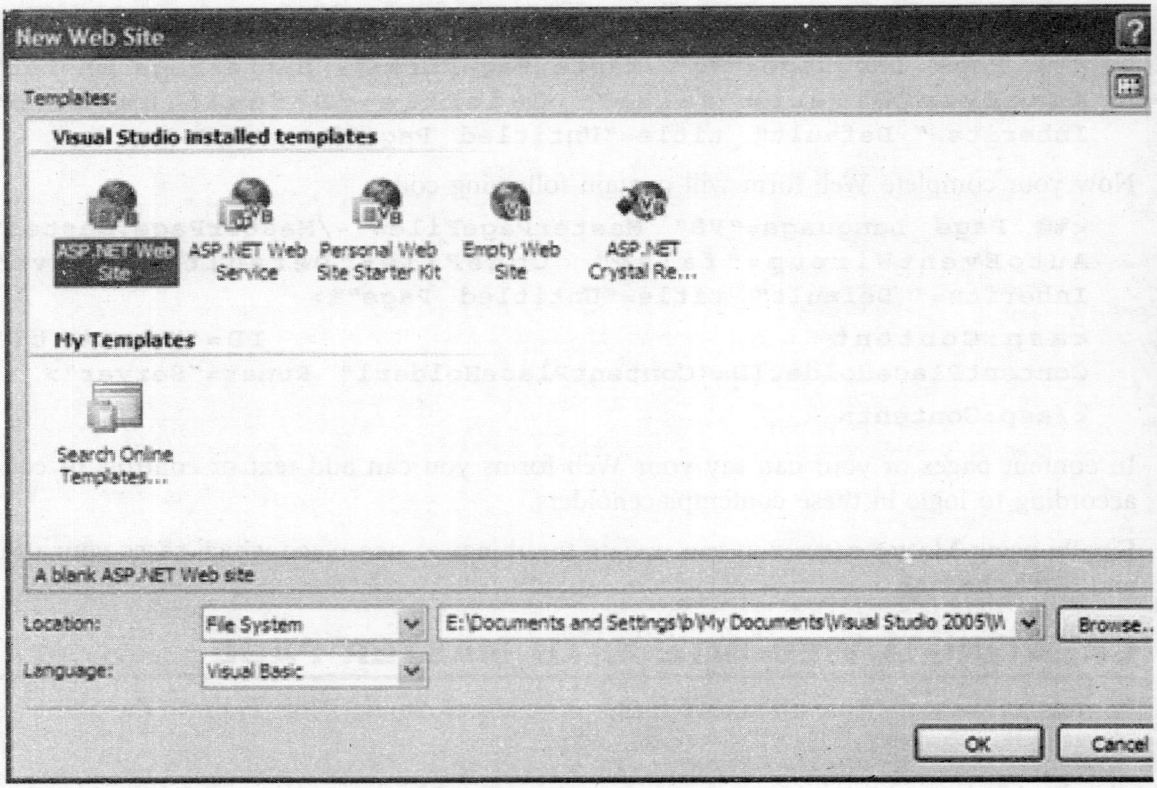

9. Right-click on Default.aspx.
10. Click Delete.
11. Dialog box appears:

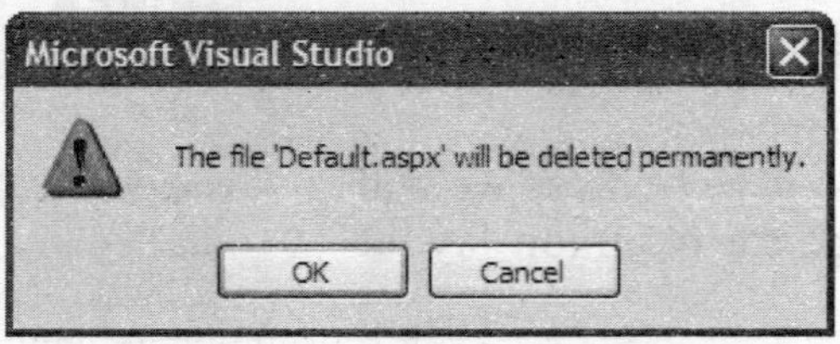

12. Click on OK button.

    Now your Solution Explorer window without any Web form may look like this:

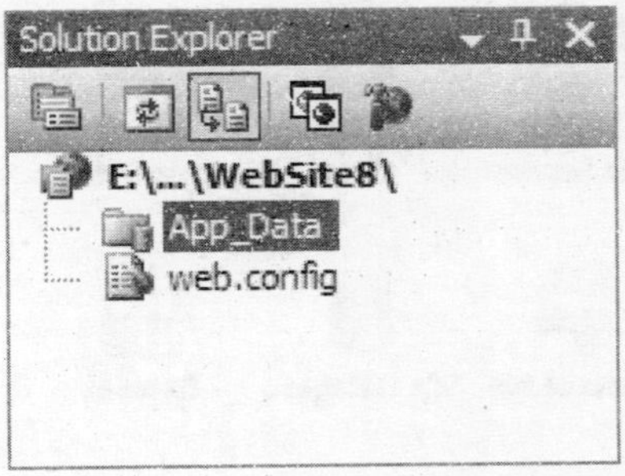

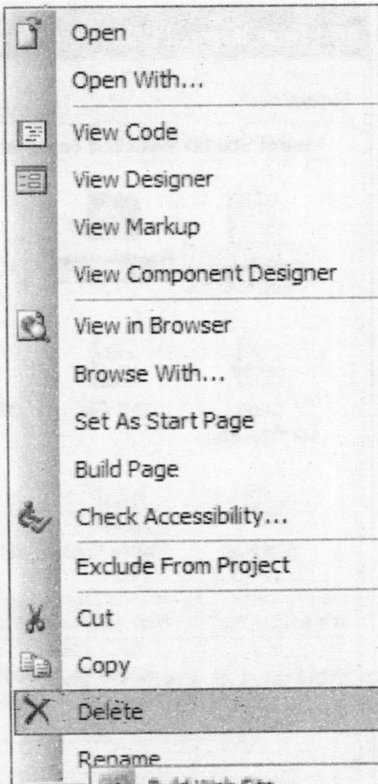

Now this is the right time to add master page for this perform the following steps:

13. Right-click the project name and click on Add New Item.. option.
14. Add New Item dialog box appears:
15. Under Templates select Master Page.
16. Keep default name in Name: field i.e. MasterPage.master.
17. In Language field select Visual Basic or any desired language.
18. Select the Place code in separate file option this will place the code in a separate file.
19. Click on Add button.
20. Master page has been added to your Web site.

    At present your Solution Explorer window may look like this with Master page added to it:

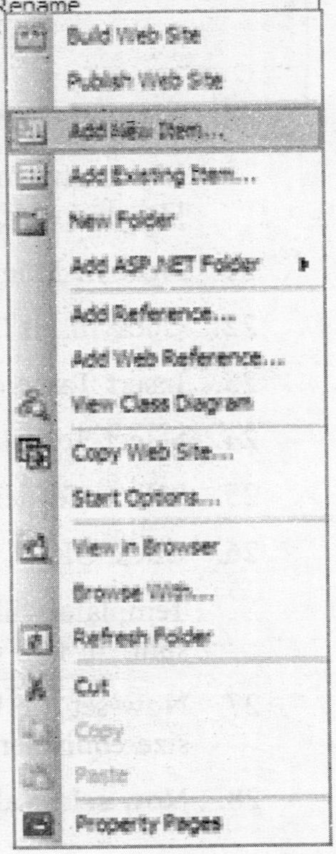

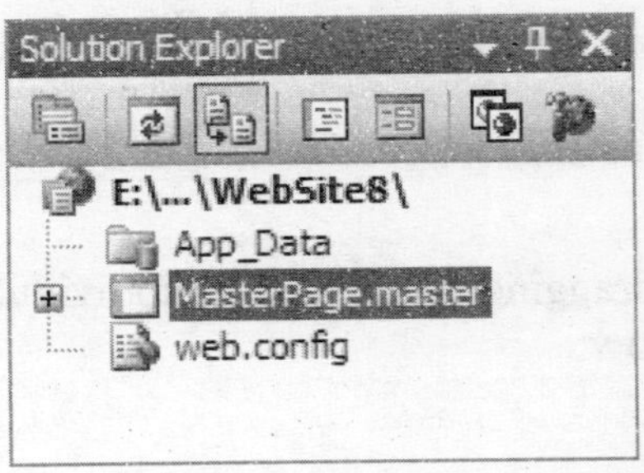

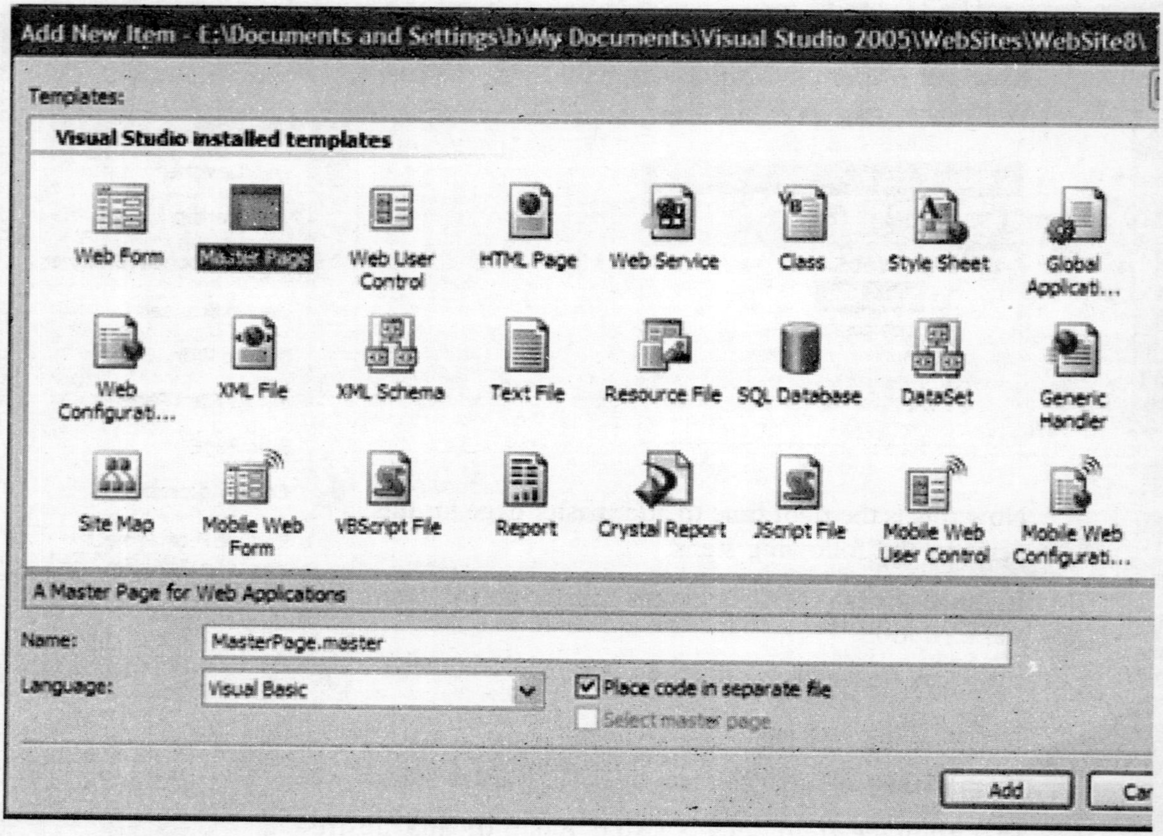

If you switch to design view your Master page may look like this with one ContentPlaceHolder control added to it:

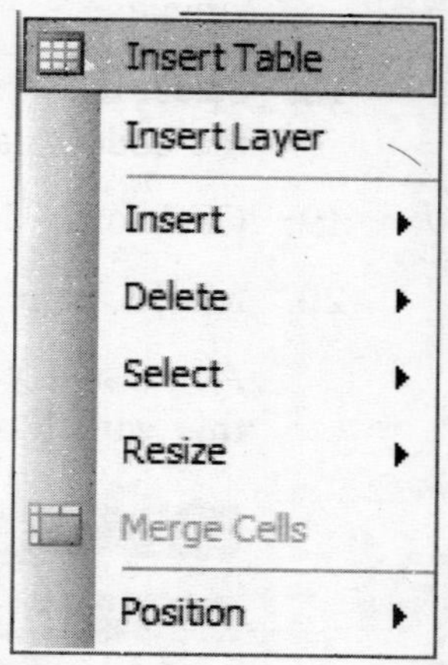

21. Now in Menu bar click Layout.
22. Click Insert Table option.
23. Insert Table dialog box appears:
24. Select Template option.
25. Select Header, footer and side option.
26. Click OK.

    Template will create three rows. Where as middle row is split in two cells.

27. Now set the height of all three rows by dragging there borders individually to the size equivalent to as shown in figure below:
28. Now select all cells.

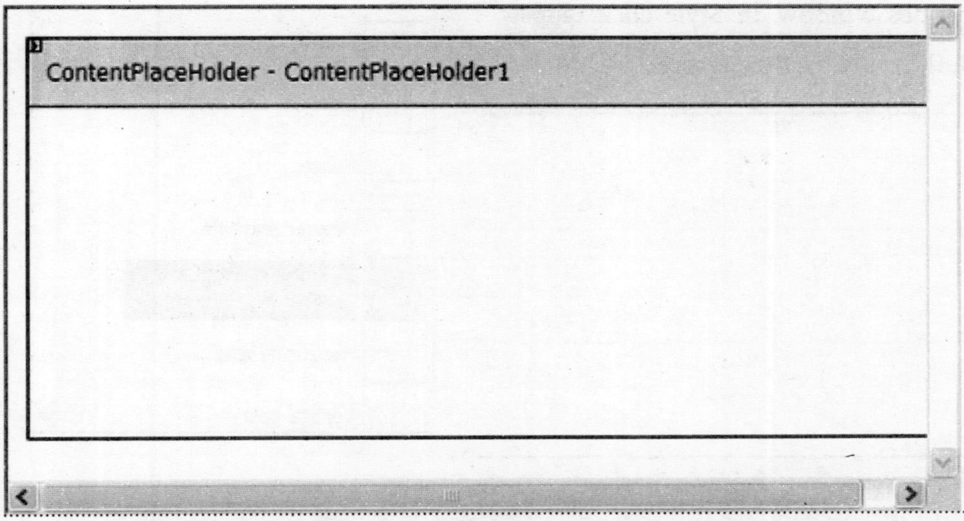
ContentPlaceHolder - ContentPlaceHolder1

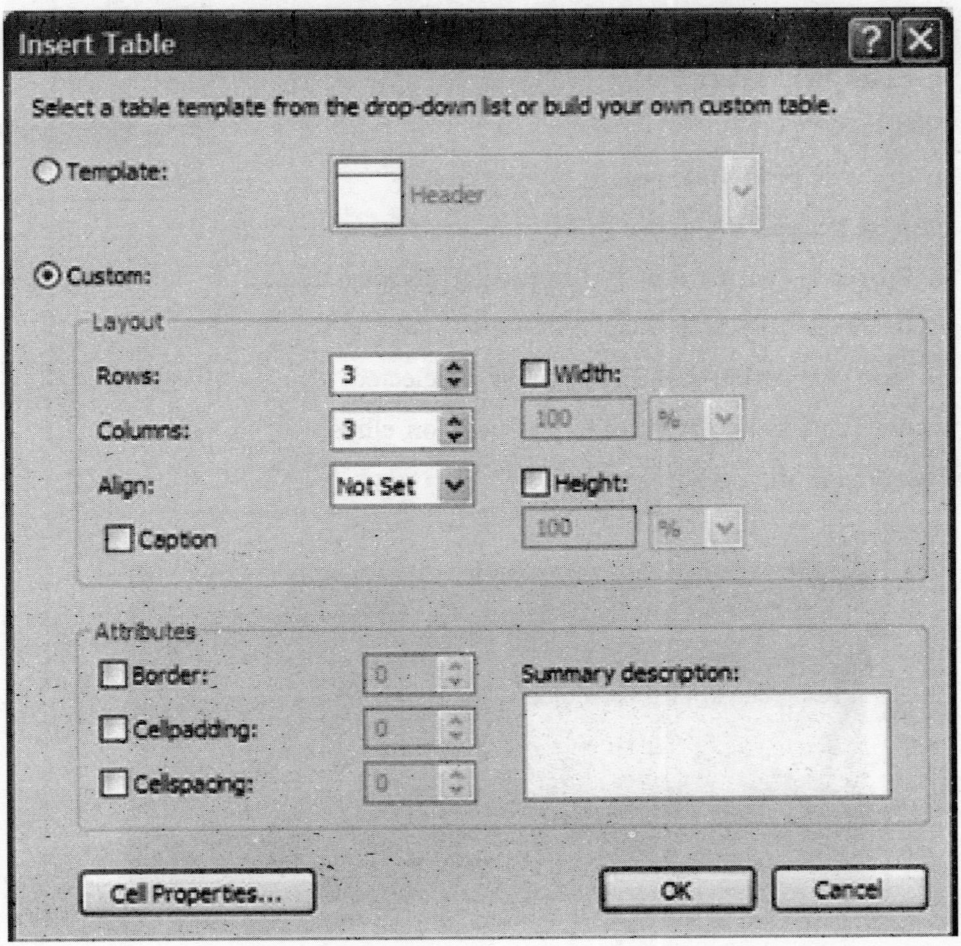
Insert Table
Select a table template from the drop-down list or build your own custom table.
Template:
Header
Custom:
Layout
Rows:
3
Columns:
3
Align:
Not Set
Caption
Width:
100
%
Height:
100
%
Attributes
Border:
0
Cellpadding:
0
Cellspacing:
0
Summary description:
Cell Properties...
OK
Cancel

29. In Properties window, in Style click ellipse
30. Style Builder dialog box appears:

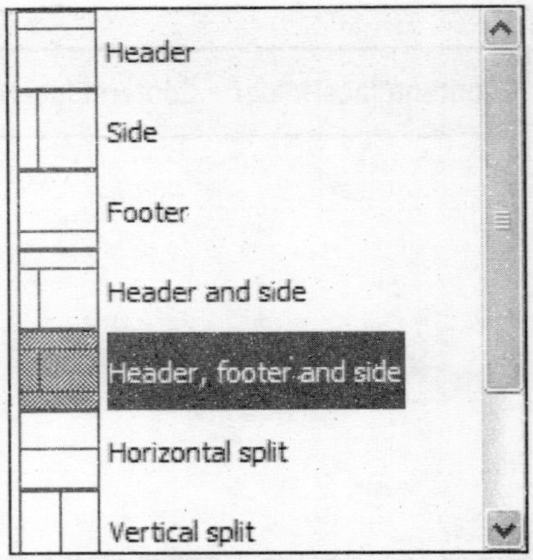

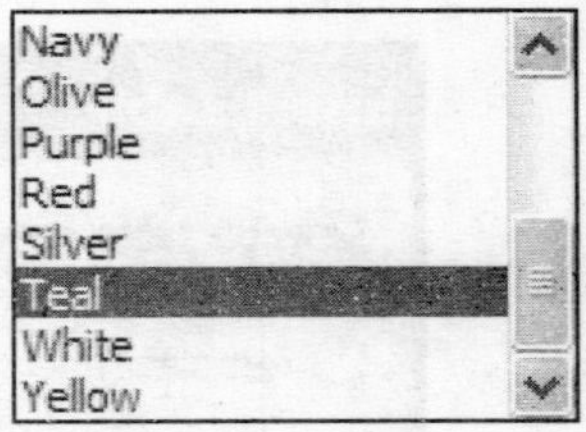

31. Select Background.
32. In Color field select Teal.
33. Click OK.
34. In top row type Welcome to Mysite.com.
35. Now select the Welcome to Mysite.com text.
36. In Properties window, in Style property click on ellipse.
37. Style Builder dialog box appears.
38. Be sure that at left side Font option is selected.
39. Under Font name, In Family field click on ellipse.
40. Font Picker dialog box appears.

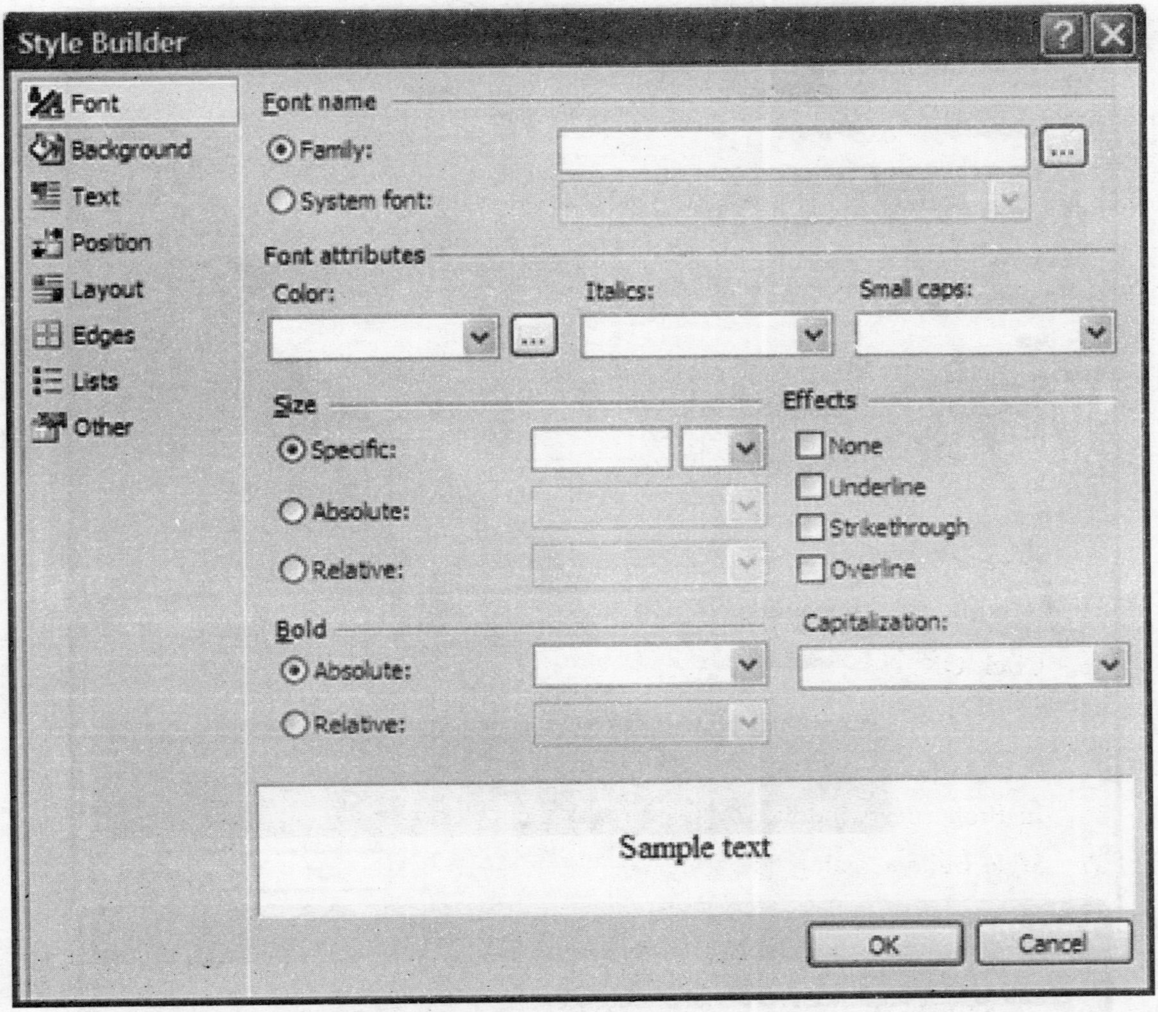

41. Select Arial and then click on >>
42. Click OK.
43. You will be back to Style Builder dialog box.
44. Under Font Attributes, select font color in Color field.
45. Select White.
46. Under Size, be sure that Specific field is selected.
47. Choose 30 Pt.
48. In Effects select Underline.
49. Under Bold field, be sure that Absolute is selected.

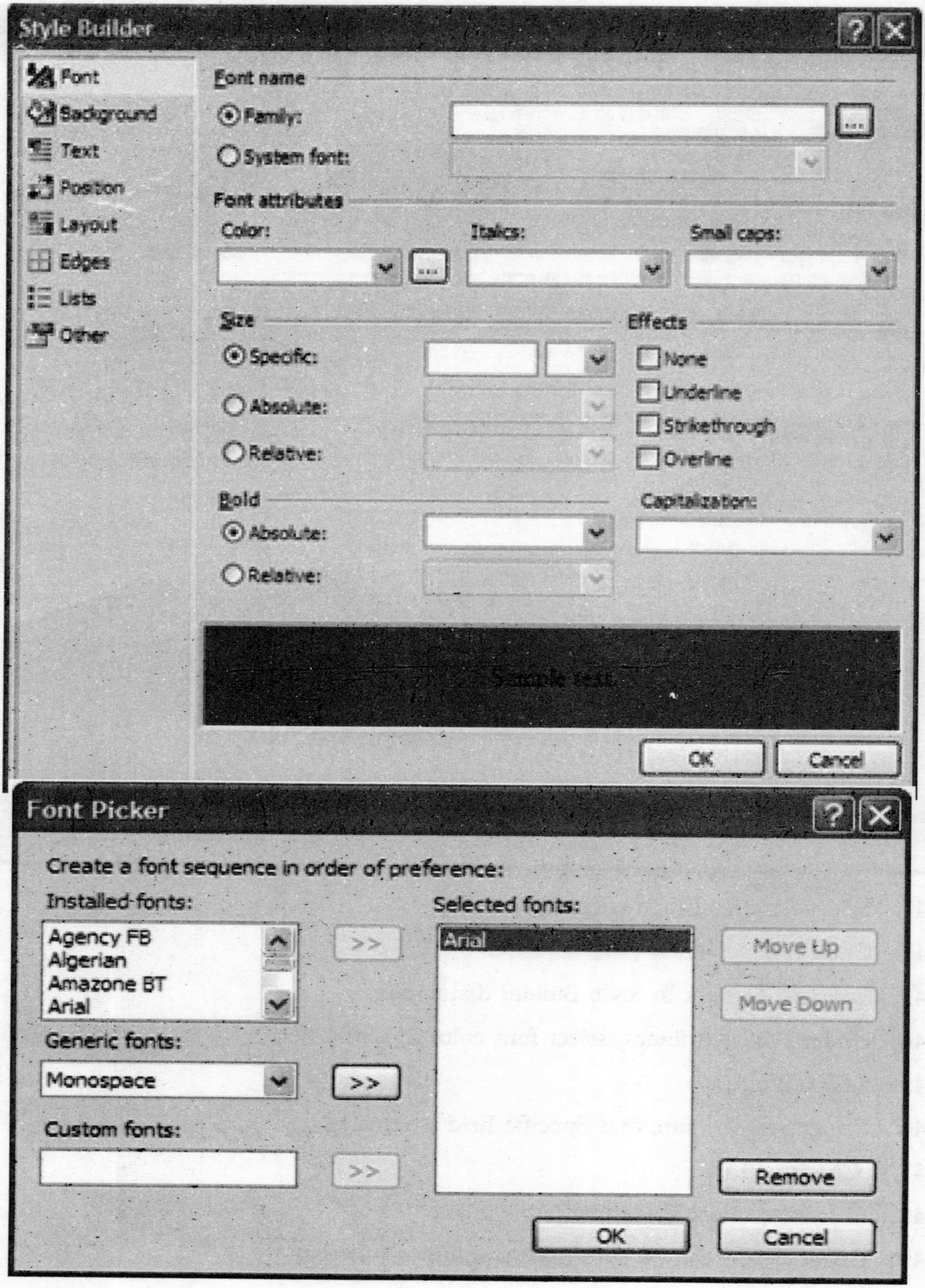
Style Builder
Font
Background
Text
Position
Layout
Edges
Lists
Other
Font name
Family:
System font:
Font attributes
Color:
Italics:
Small caps:
Size
Specific:
Absolute:
Relative:
Effects
None
Underline
Strikethrough
Overline
Bold
Absolute:
Relative:
Capitalization:
OK
Cancel
Font Picker
Create a font sequence in order of preference:
Installed fonts:
Agency FB
Algerian
Amazone BT
Arial
Generic fonts:
Monospace
Custom fonts:
Selected fonts:
Arial
Move Up
Move Down
Remove
OK
Cancel

50. Select Bold.

51. You may see the preview of whole at bottom.

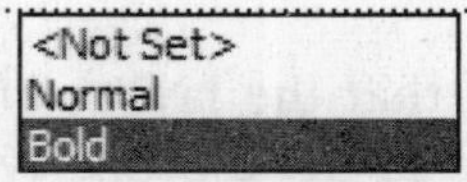

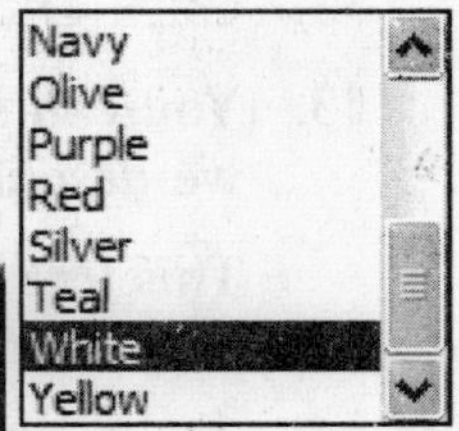

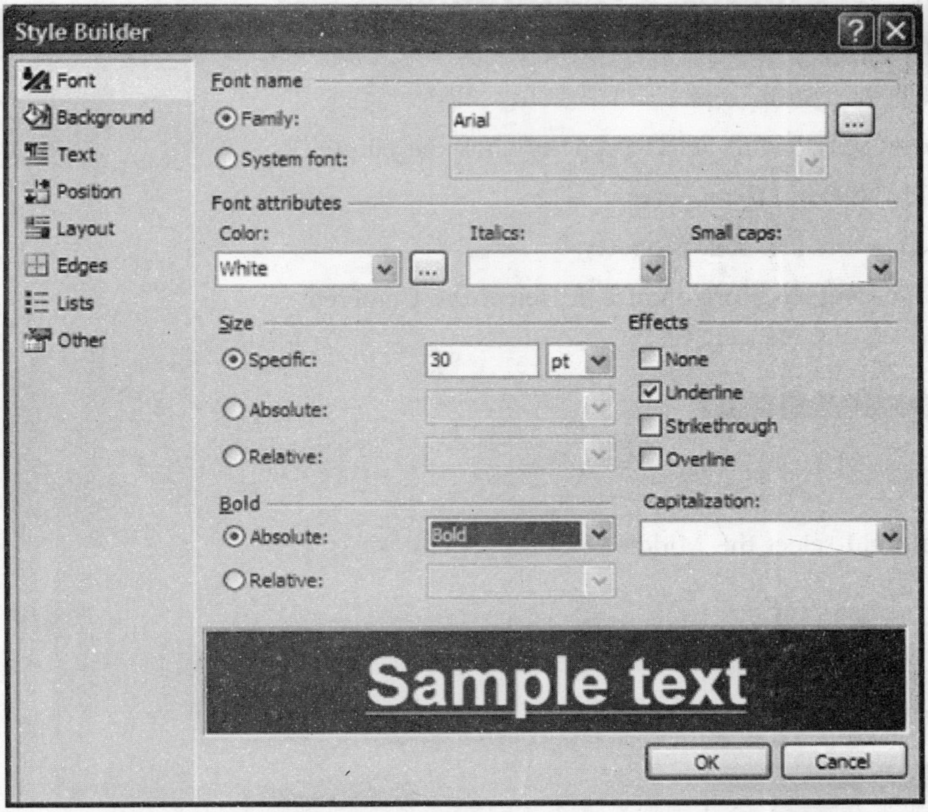

52. Click OK.
53. You can see that the layout of text at top row has been changed to new one as we described in Style property.

    This text is left aligned for better visibility and look let we set it to center. For this perform the following steps:
54. Again select the whole text.
55. In Properties window, in Select property click the ellipse.
56. Style Builder dialog box appears.
57. At left side select the Text property.
58. Under Alignment, in Horizontal field select the Centered.

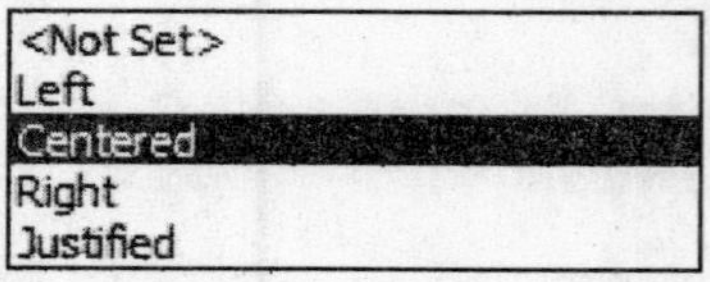

59. In Vertical field select the Middle option.

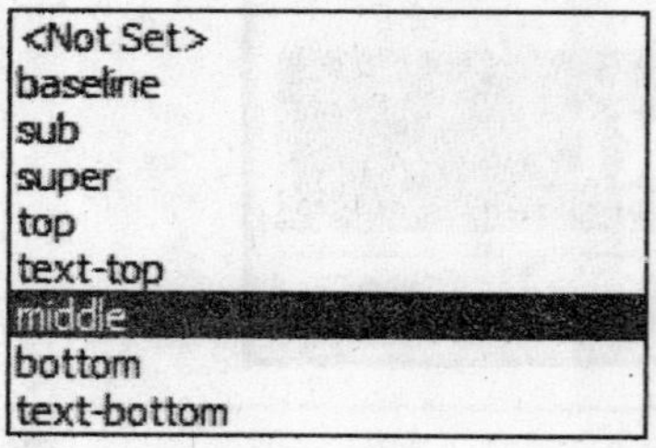

60. Under Spacing between, in Letters field select Normal.

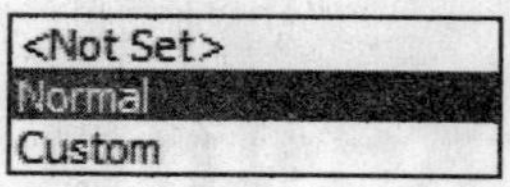

61. In Lines field select Normal.

62. You can see the preview at the bottom of the dialog-box.

At this stage the whole Style Builder dialog box will look like the one shown below.

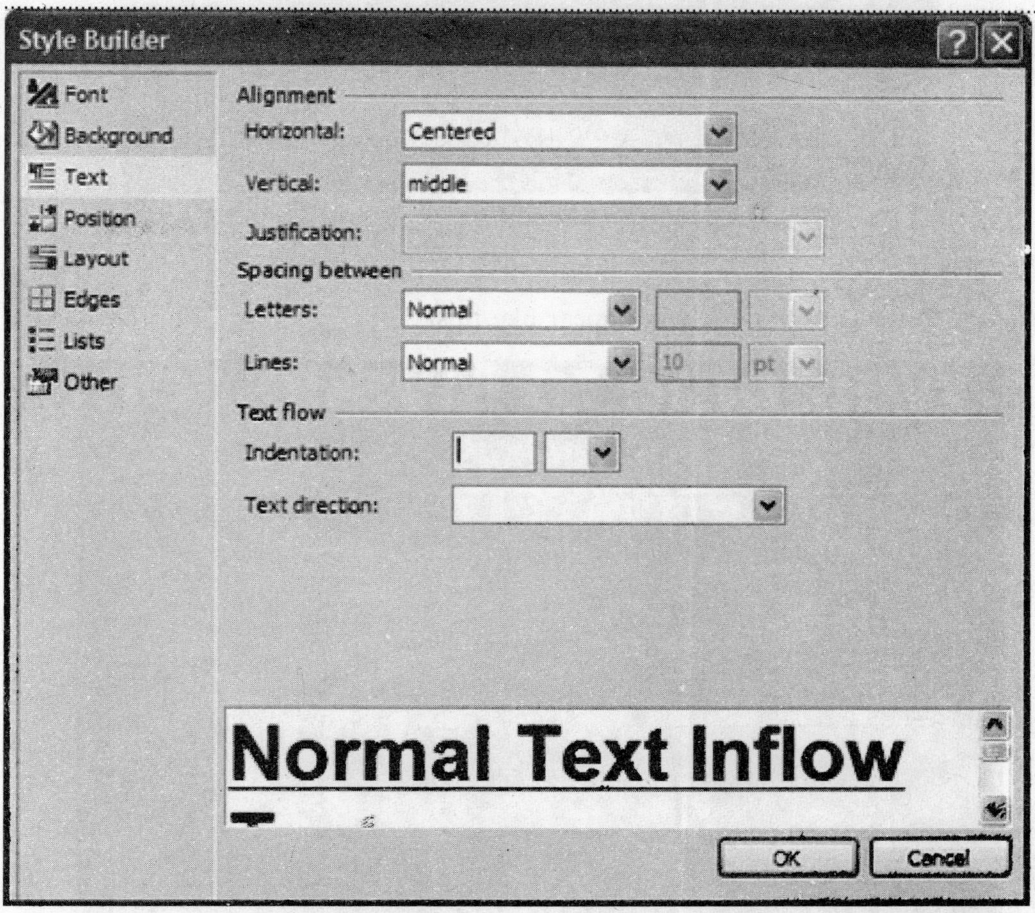

63. Now click OK button.
64. You may notice this that text has been aligned center.
65. Now in second row in first cell type following text:
    - About Us
    - Products
    - Online Purchase

• Contact Us

66. At this stage the table will appear like this:

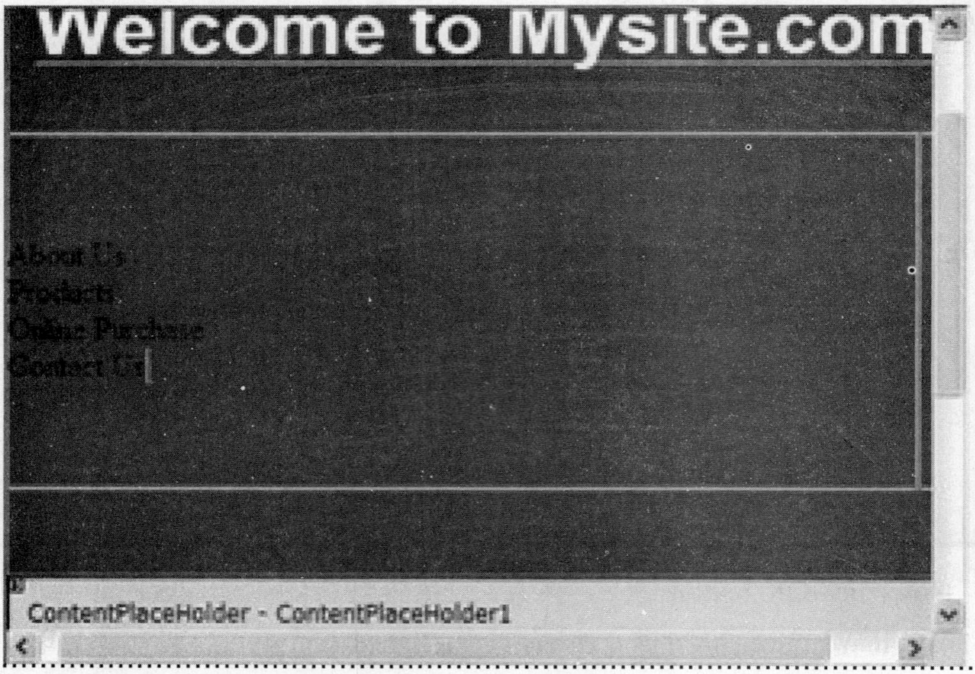

67. Now drag the ContentPlaceHolder control in the second cell of second row.
68. At this stage the table will appear like this:
69. Now click on third row and type “Copyright @ Mysite.com

Notice here that this complete master page is a common layout for your all Web forms.

The role of first row is to display the Web site name. Second row plays two roles one is the first cell is a common layout of links for all Web forms and second cell is the place where all Web forms can manipulate and text or other stuffs according to page requirement. Third role will display the copyright information in all Web forms or Web pages.

Now your complete master page will look like this:

Like this you can design the common layout of your Website using master page.

Now this is the right time to implement this master page in our new Web page or Web form.

CONTENT CREATION USING MASTER PAGE

When you add ASP.net page of Web form page to your Website you basically define the content for master page but for this you have to associate this page with master page.

For this perform the following steps:

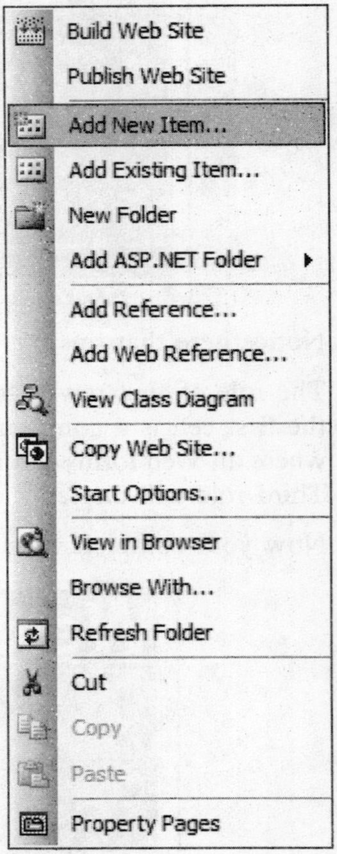

1. In Solution Explorer window right-click thè project name.
2. Click on Add New Item..
3. Add New dialog box appears.
4. Select Web Form.
5. In Name: field keep default name Default.aspx which is a first page of your Web site.
6. In Language field select Visual Basic you can also choose any other desired language.
7. Be sure that Place code in separate file option is checked.
8. Below it check the Select Master page option
9. Click on Add button.
10. Select a Master Page dialog box appears.
11. Under Contents of folder: select the MasterPage.master.
12. Click OK button.
13. If you see the source of Default.aspx page then you will find such code generated by Visual Studio.

```
<%@ Page Language="VB" MasterPageFile="~/MasterPage.master"
AutoEventWireup="false" CodeFile="Default.aspx.vb"
Inherits="_Default" title="Untitled Page"%>
<%– Add content controls here –%>
```

14. Switch to Design view and be sure that Default.aspx page is selected in Solution Explorer window.

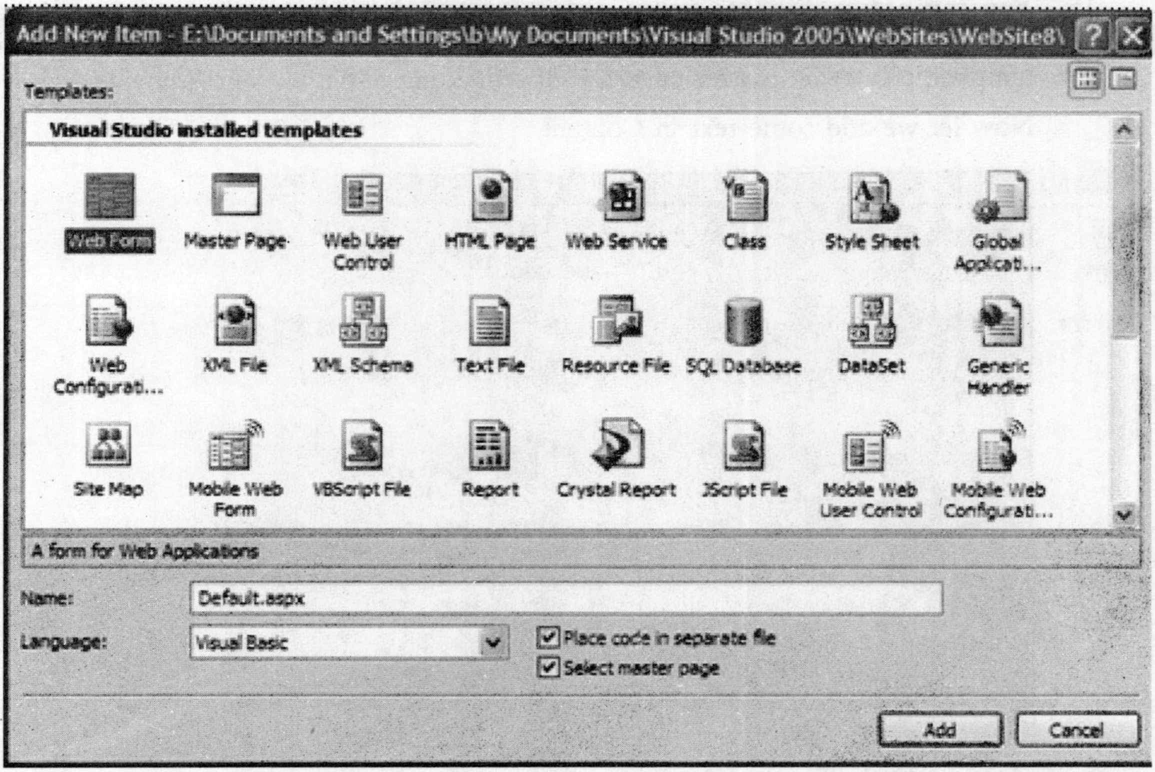
Add New Item - E:\Documents and Settings\b\My Documents\Visual Studio 2005\WebSites\WebSite8\
Templates:
Visual Studio installed templates
Web Form
Master Page
Web User Control
HTML Page
Web Service
Class
Style Sheet
Global Applicati...
Web Configurati...
XML File
XML Schema
Text File
Resource File
SQL Database
DataSet
Generic Handler
Site Map
Mobile Web Form
VBScript File
Report
Crystal Report
JScript File
Mobile Web User Control
Mobile Web Configurati...
A form for Web Applications
Name:
Default.aspx
Language:
Visual Basic
Place code in separate file
Select master page
Add
Cancel

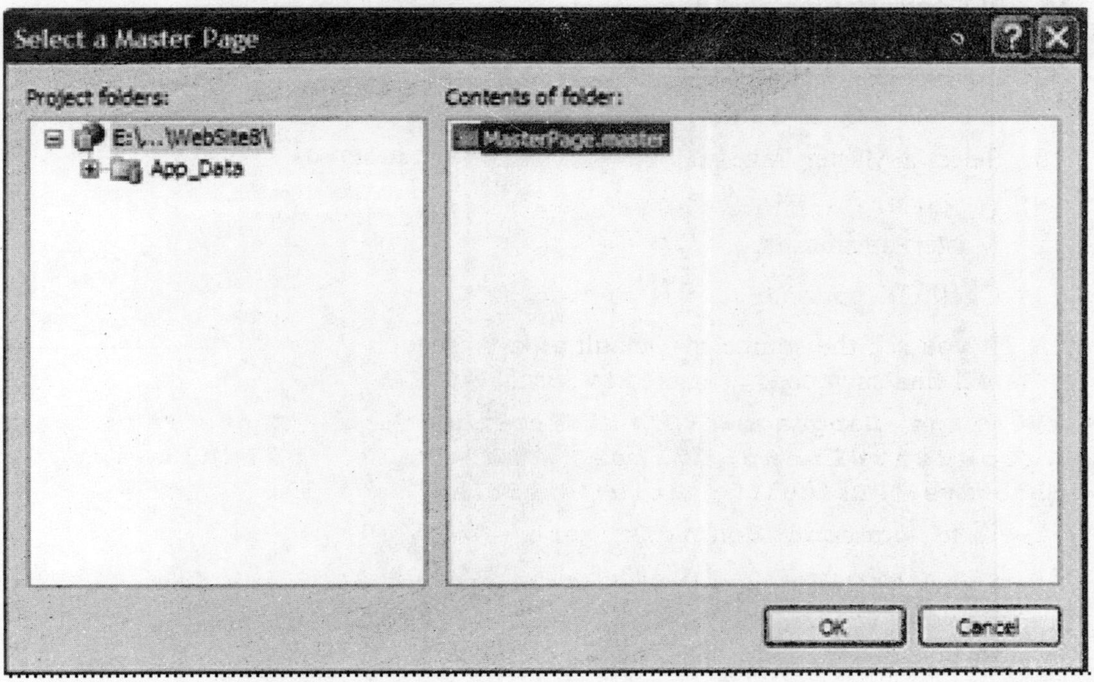
Select a Master Page
Project folders:
Contents of folder:
E:\...\WebSite8\
App_Data
MasterPage.master
OK
Cancel

15. You can notice this that only Content control portion is active and remaining portion is dimmed means you can not edit them because these are fixed layout of template created in master page for all remaining pages in your Web site.

    Now let we add some text in Content.

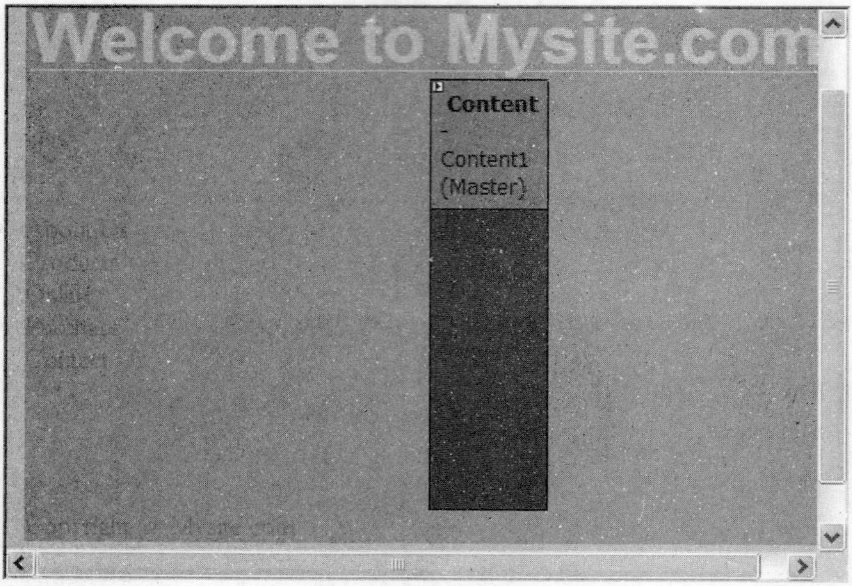

16. In Content at top click the triangle.

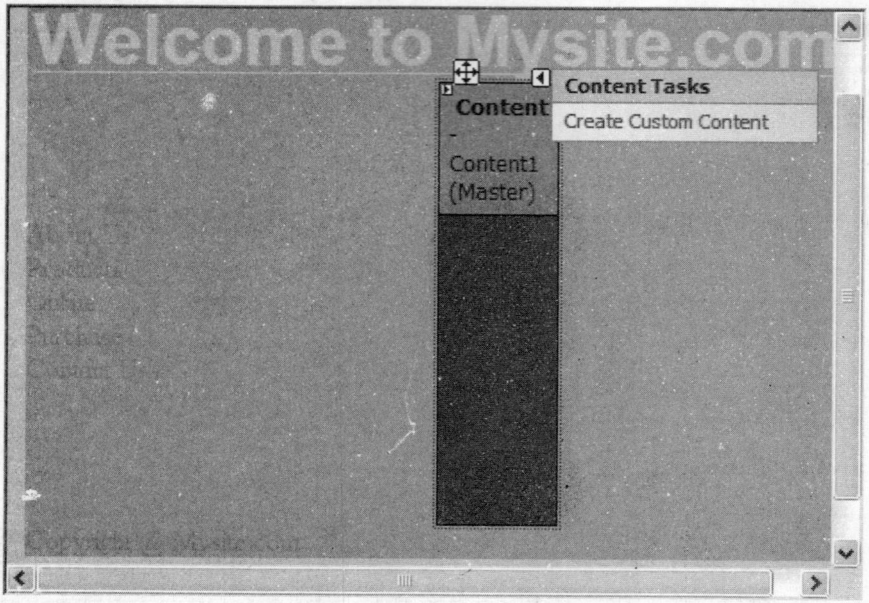

17. Now click on Create Custom Content.
18. Type “We basically deals in Online Sales and Purchase of products.”

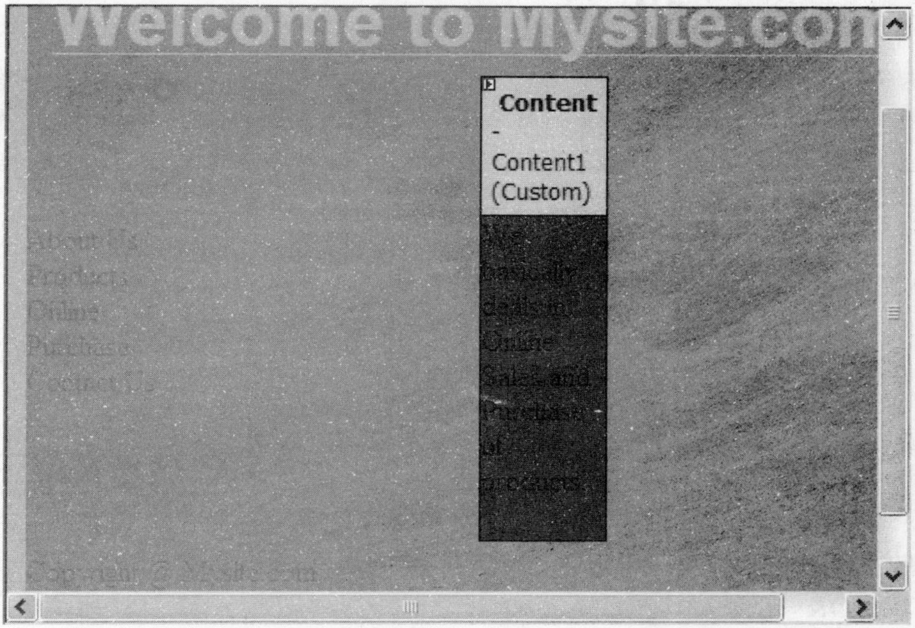

Now if we see the source code then you will notice this that automatically Content control has been added with text.

```
<%@ Page Language="VB" MasterPageFile="~/MasterPage.master"
AutoEventWireup="false" CodeFile="Default.aspx.vb"
Inherits="_Default" title="Untitled Page"%>
<%— Add content controls here —%>
<asp:Content ID="Content1" runat="server"
ContentPlaceHolderID="ContentPlaceHolder1">
     <span style="font-size: 12pt; color: black; font-family:
'Times New Roman'; mso-fareast-font-family: 'Times New Roman';
          mso-ansi-language: EN-US; mso-fareast-language: EN-
US; mso-bidi-language: AR-SA">
          We basically deal in Online Sales and Purchase of
products.</span></asp:Content>
```

Now this is the right time to run the Web site.

1. For this click on the Start button at top.

2. Debugging Not Enabled dialog box appears:

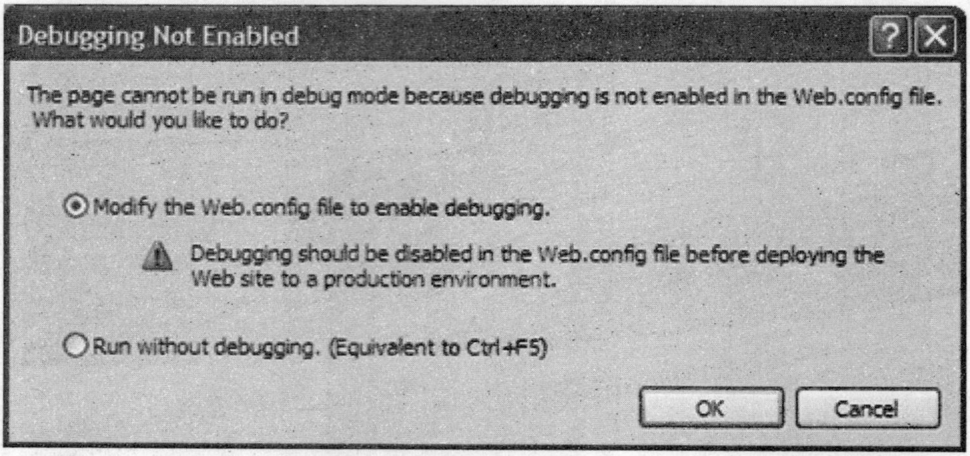

3. Select the second option Run without debugging. (Equivalent to Ctrl + F5)
4. Click OK.

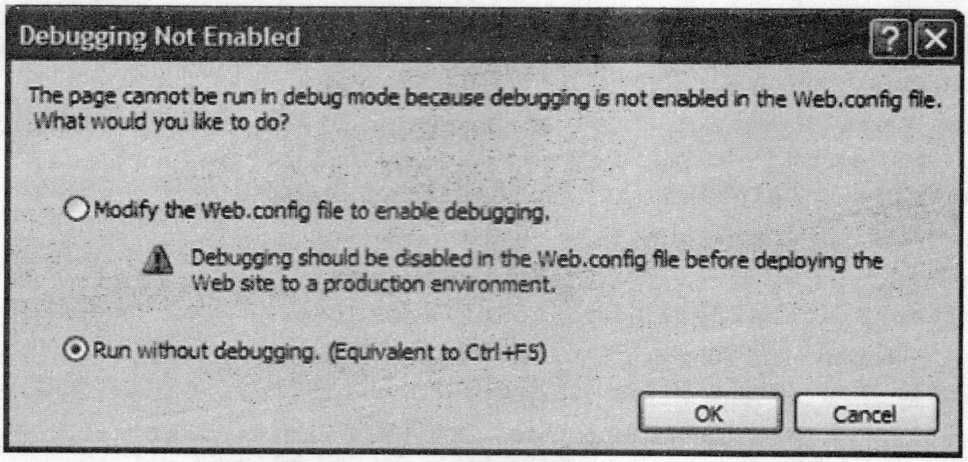

5. You will find the following output in Web browser:

You will notice this that header, footer and links at left side are automatically generated through master page.

CSS AND ASP

It is obvious that your Web site should look and feel good. Everything related to appearance is designed using colors, and many other type of formatting options. Compare to HTML,

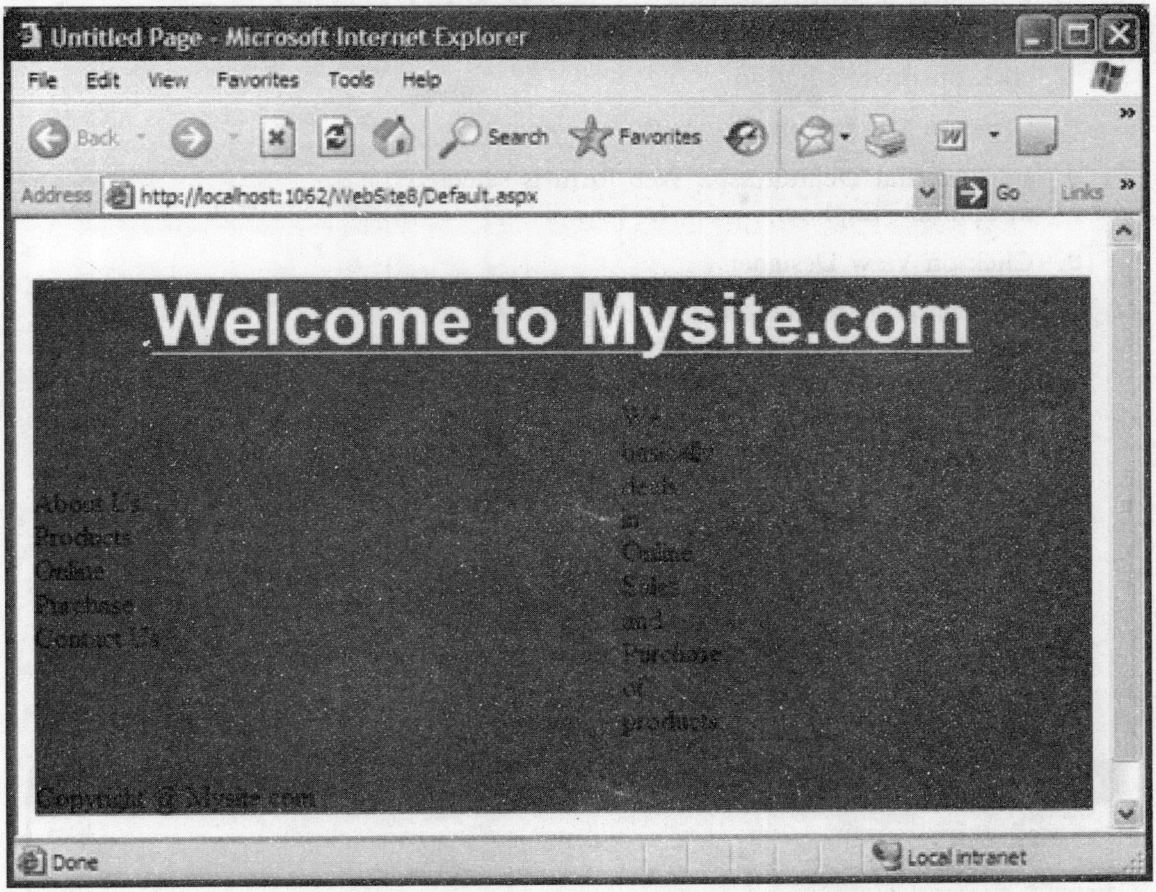

CSS provides much more uniformity and easiness to design good looking Web site or Web page.

In Visual Studio you can implement CSS in no-time and can easily integrate with ASP.NET pages.

Let we first create the Web site, for this perform the following steps:

1. Click on the File menu.
2. Click New Web Site…
3. New Web Site dialog box appears.
4. Under Templates: select ASP.NET Web Site.
5. In Location: field, choose File System.
6. In Language: field, choose Visual Basic, you can also choose other languages like Visual C# or Visual J#.

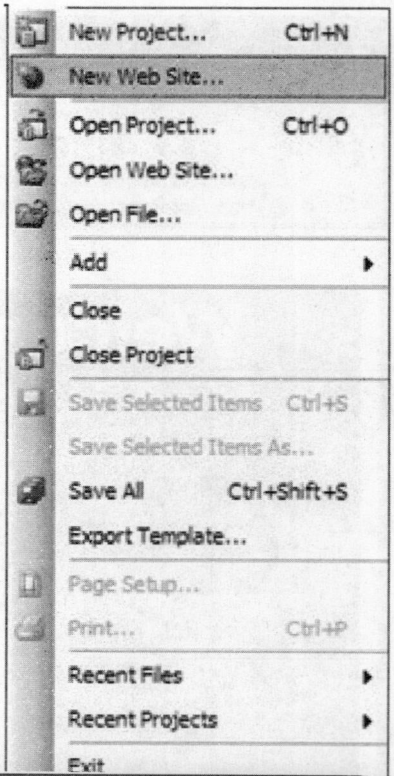

7. Keep default Web site name generated by Visual Studio. To specify different location and name click on Browse button.
8. Click on OK button.
9. Be sure that Default.aspx Web form is selected in Solution Explorer.
10. Click on View Designer.
11. You will jump to Design view, in Center Window of your default.aspx page click inside at top and type "Hello World this is my Web page".

    Let we run it and see at present how it looks in a Web browser.
12. At top bar click on Start Debugging button.
13. Debugging Not Enabled dialog box appears.

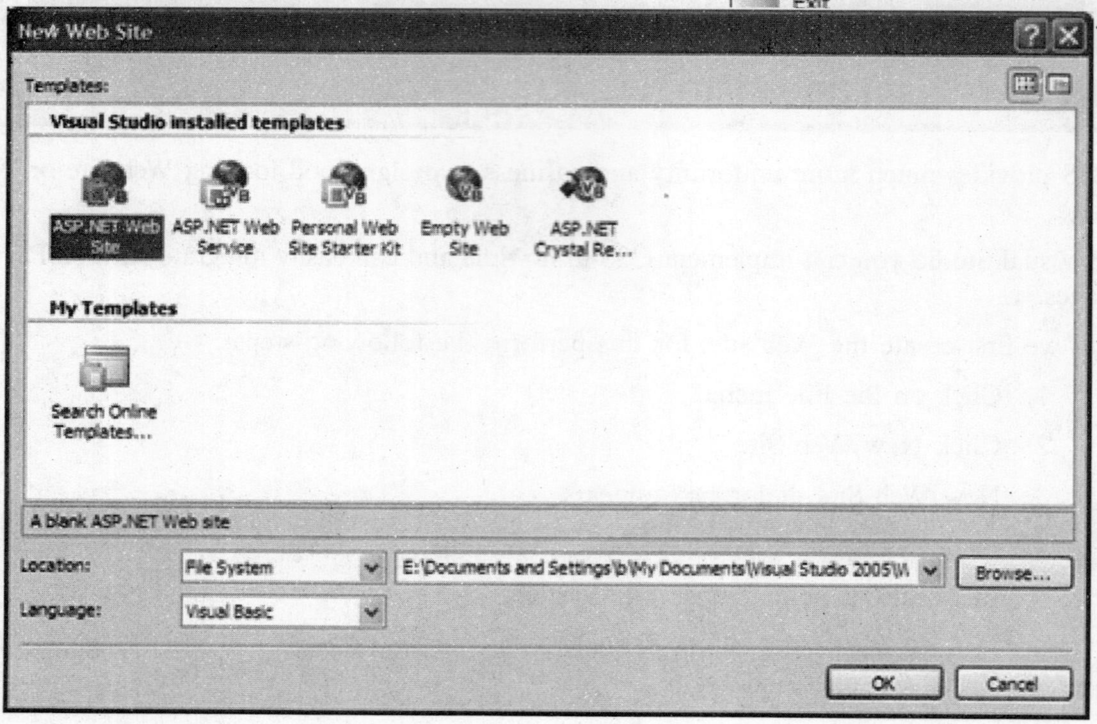

14. Select the second option Run without debugging. (Equivalent to Ctrl + F5)

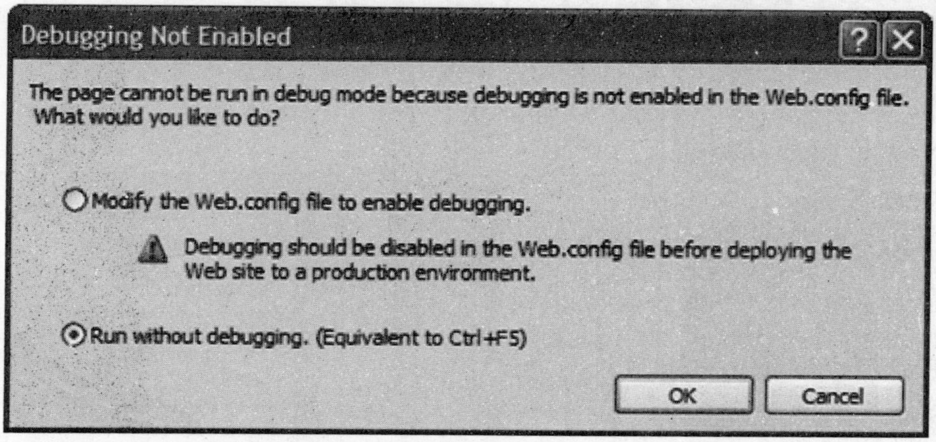

15. Now click on OK button.

You will find the following output in a Web browser:

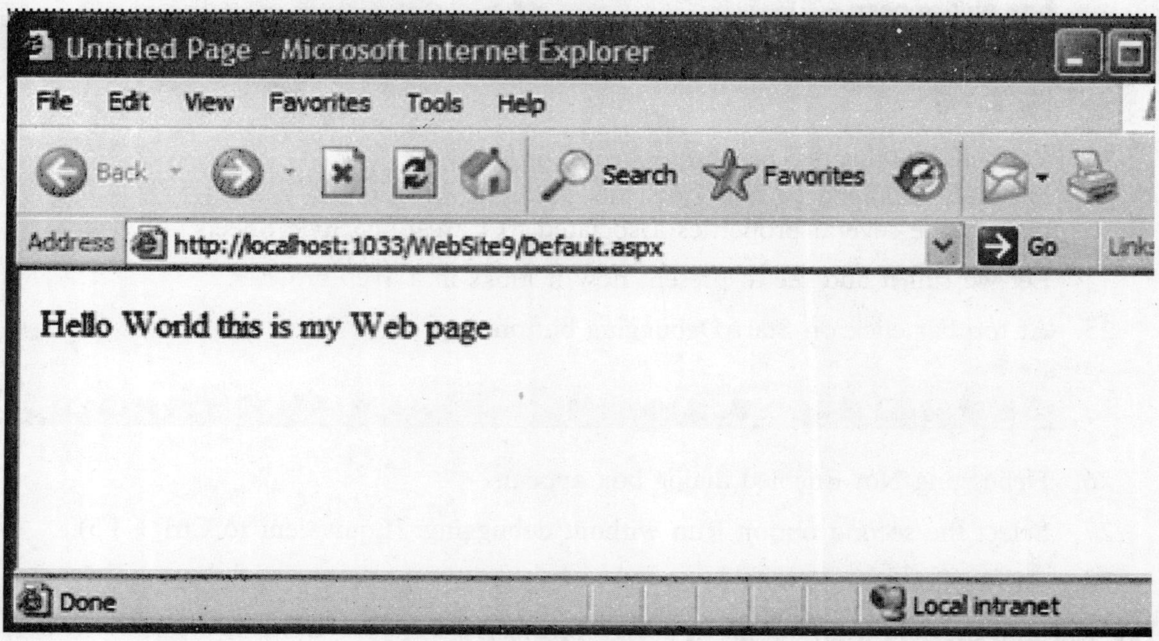

This is very basic layout. Using Style Sheets we can format the page in better appearance. Now switch back to Visual Studio by closing this browser.

Be sure that your cursor is active in Design view inside the default.aspx page in center as shown in figure below:

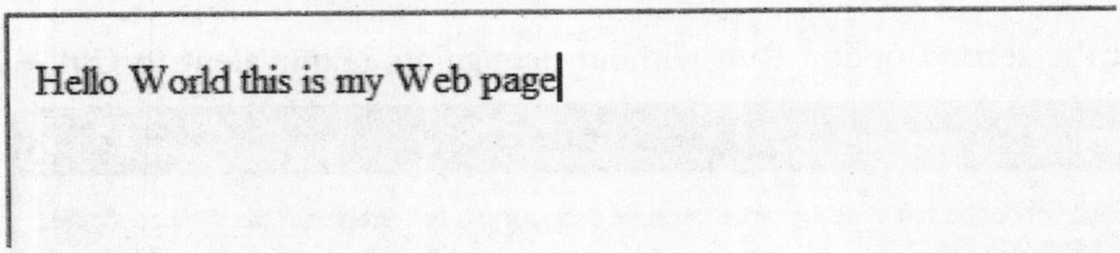

16. Now in menu bar click Format.
17. Click Style....

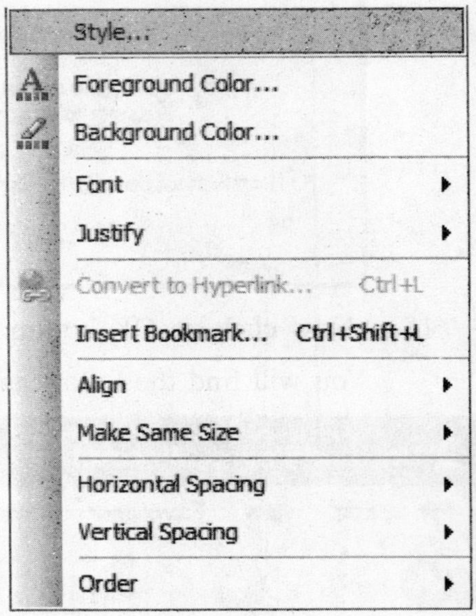

18. Style Builder dialog box will appear.

    Here you can set all designing aspects related to your text like Font, Background, Text, Position, Layout, Edges, Lists etc.
19. Select Background.
20. Click on Ellipse next to Color field.
21. You will notice this that Color Picker dialog box will appear.
22. Select Red color.
23. Click OK.
24. You will find this that background color of text has been changed to red. Like this you can manipulate several properties associated to Cascading Style Sheets.

    Let we run it and see at present how it looks in a Web browser.
25. At top bar click on Start Debugging button.

26. Debugging Not Enabled dialog box appears.
27. Select the second option Run without debugging. (Equivalent to Ctrl + F5)
28. Now click on OK button.

You will find the following output in a Web browser:

This time the background color is different.

Visual Studio has automatically created the style sheet and attached it with the text:

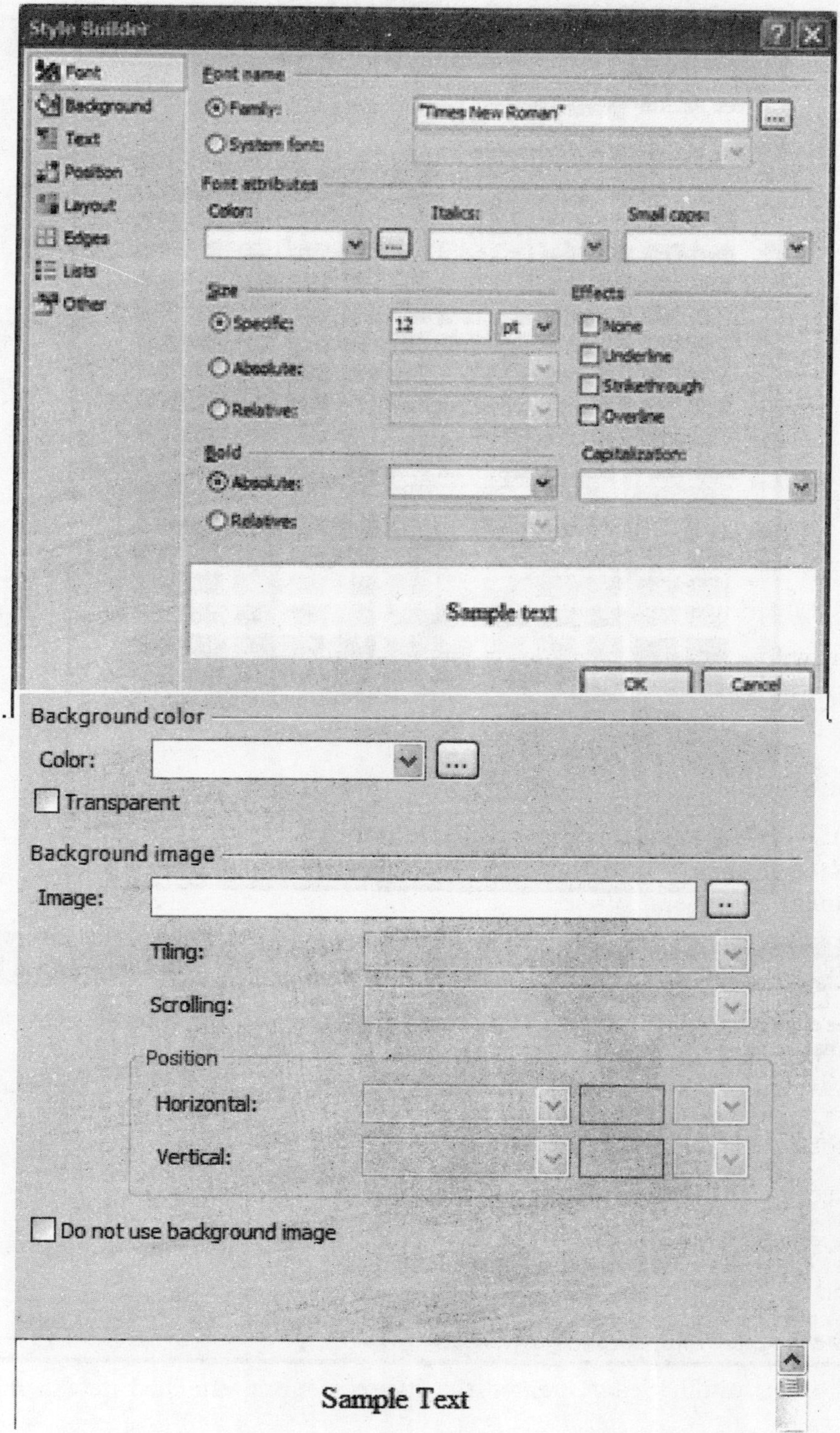
Style Builder
Font
Background
Text
Position
Layout
Edges
Lists
Other
Font name
Family:
"Times New Roman"
System font:
Font attributes
Color:
Italics:
Small caps:
Size
Specific:
12
pt
Absolute:
Relative:
Effects
None
Underline
Strikethrough
Overline
Bold
Absolute:
Relative:
Capitalization:
Sample text
OK
Cancel
Background color
Color:
Transparent
Background image
Image:
Tiling:
Scrolling:
Position
Horizontal:
Vertical:
Do not use background image
Sample Text

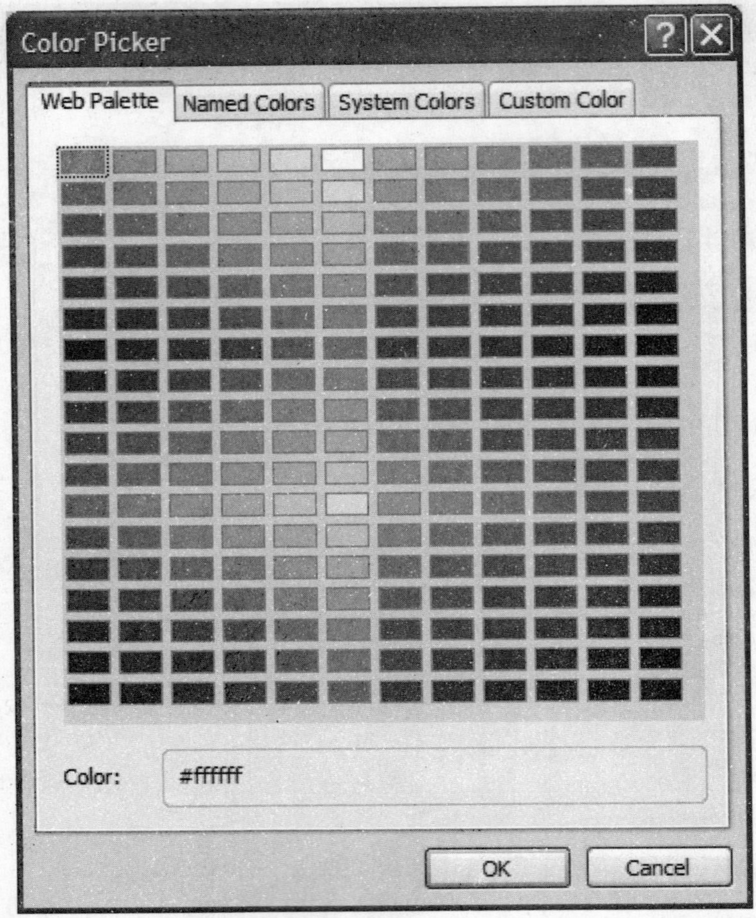
Color Picker
Web Palette
Named Colors
System Colors
Custom Color
Color:
#ffffff
OK
Cancel

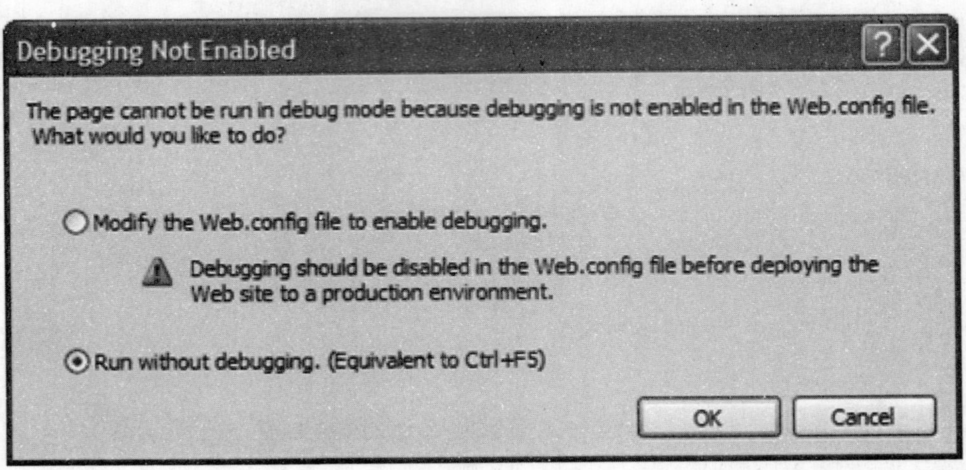
Debugging Not Enabled
The page cannot be run in debug mode because debugging is not enabled in the Web.config file. What would you like to do?
Modify the Web.config file to enable debugging.
Debugging should be disabled in the Web.config file before deploying the Web site to a production environment.
Run without debugging. (Equivalent to Ctrl+F5)
OK
Cancel

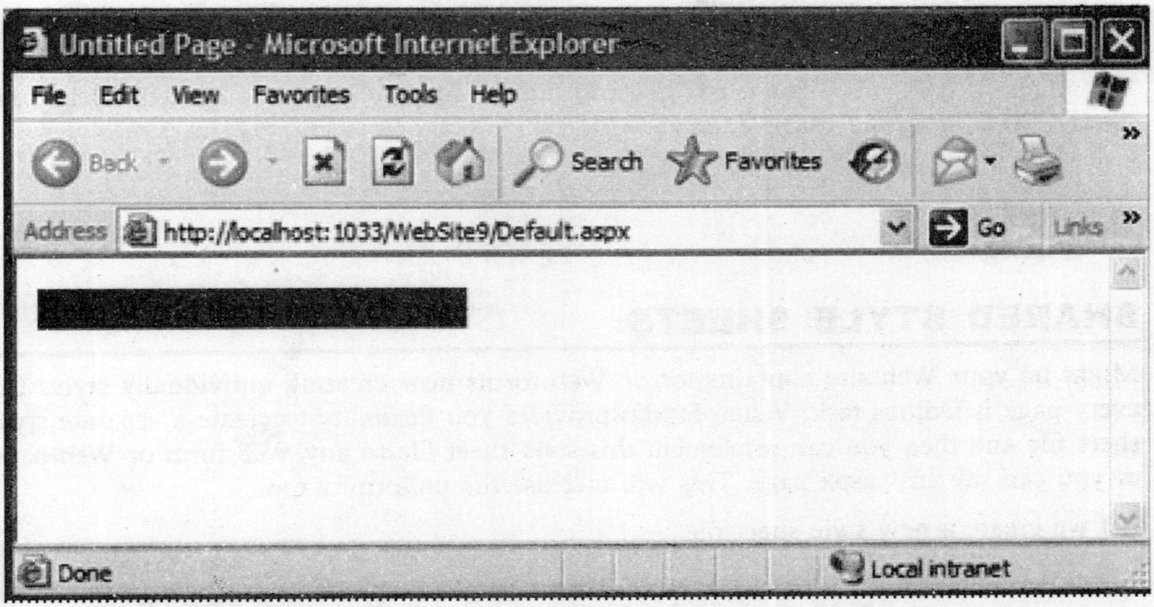


```
<span style="font-size: 12pt; font-family: 'Times New Roman'; background-color: #cc0000;
            mso-fareast-font-family: 'Times New Roman'; mso-ansi-language: EN-US; mso-fareast-language: EN-US;
                mso-bidi-language: AR-SA">Hello World this is my Web page</span>
```

The complete code for this default.aspx web page is like this:

```
<%@ Page Language="VB" AutoEventWireup="false" CodeFile="Default.aspx.vb" Inherits="_Default"%>
<!DOCTYPE html PUBLIC "-//W3C//DTD XHTML 1.0 Transitional//EN" "http://www.w3.org/TR/xhtml1/DTD/xhtml1-transitional.dtd">
<html xmlns="http://www.w3.org/1999/xhtml" >
<head runat="server">
    <title>Untitled Page</title>
</head>
<body>
    <form id="form1" runat="server">
    <div>
        <span style="font-size: 12pt; font-family: 'Times New Roman'; background-color: #cc0000;
```

```
                mso-fareast-font-family: 'Times New Roman'; mso-
ansi-language: EN-US; mso-fareast-language: EN-US;
                mso-bidi-language: AR-SA">Hello World this is
my Web page</span></div>
    </form>
</body>
</html>
```

SHARED STYLE SHEETS

Might be your Web site contains lot of Web forms now creating individually styles for every page is tedious task. Visual Studio provides you flexibility to create a separate style sheet file and then you can implement this style sheet file to any Web form or Web page or you can say any .aspx page. This will increase the uniformity too.

Let we create a new style sheet file.

1. Right-click in Project name in Solution Explorer window.
2. Click Add New Item.. option.
3. Add New Item dialog box appears.
4. Select Style Sheet option.
5. In Name field keep default name StyleSheet.css.
6. Now click Add button.
7. Notice in the Solution Explorer window that Style Sheet page has been added.

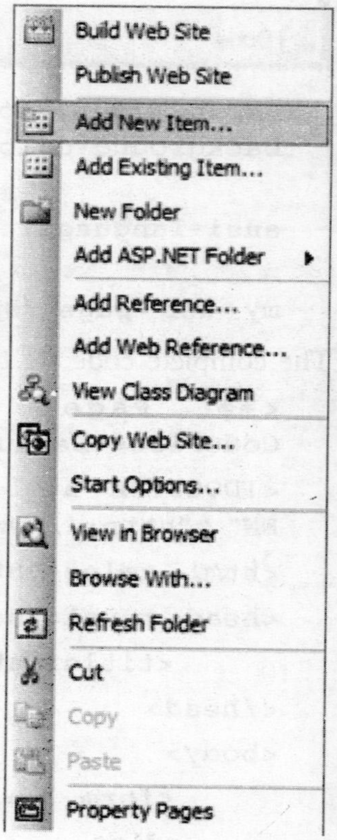

8. At present your style sheets contains the following code:

```
body
{

}
```

Now after creating a style sheet file you have to add a named style rule to a style sheet file. Web pages can refer to any style rules that the files have. Style rule is made up of name followed by a list of CSS properties and values.

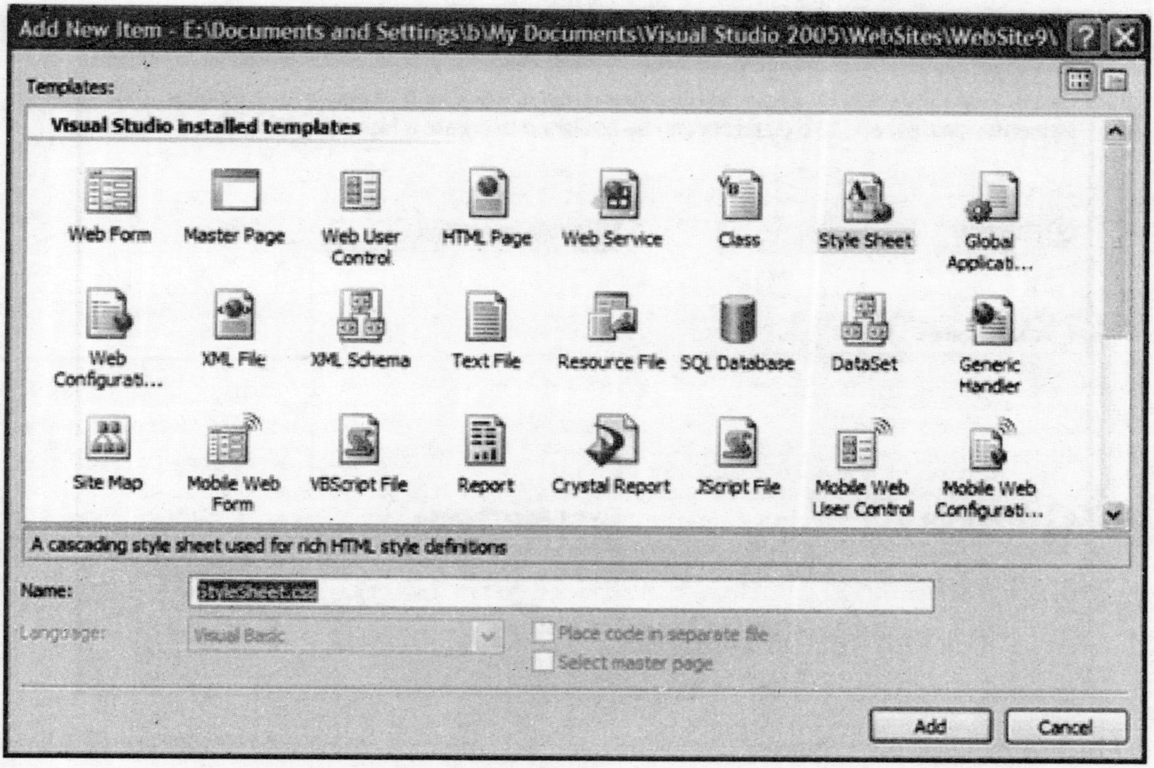

There are three types of style names:

World Wide Web Consortium	*Visual Web Developer*	*Applies to*
Type Selector	Element Name	All HTML elements
Class Selector	Class Name	All tags coded with a corresponding class = attribute
ID Selector	Element ID	All tags coded with a corresponding ID = attribute.

9. Now to add style rule in menu bar click Styles.
10. Click Add Style Rule.

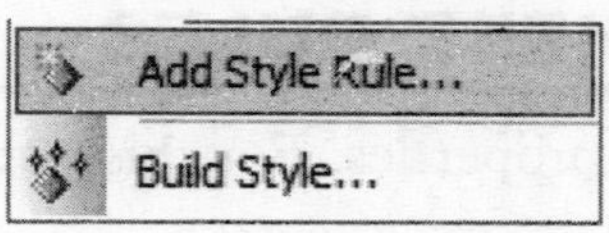

11. Add Style Rule dialog box appears:
12. Select element.
13. Select P:first-letter.

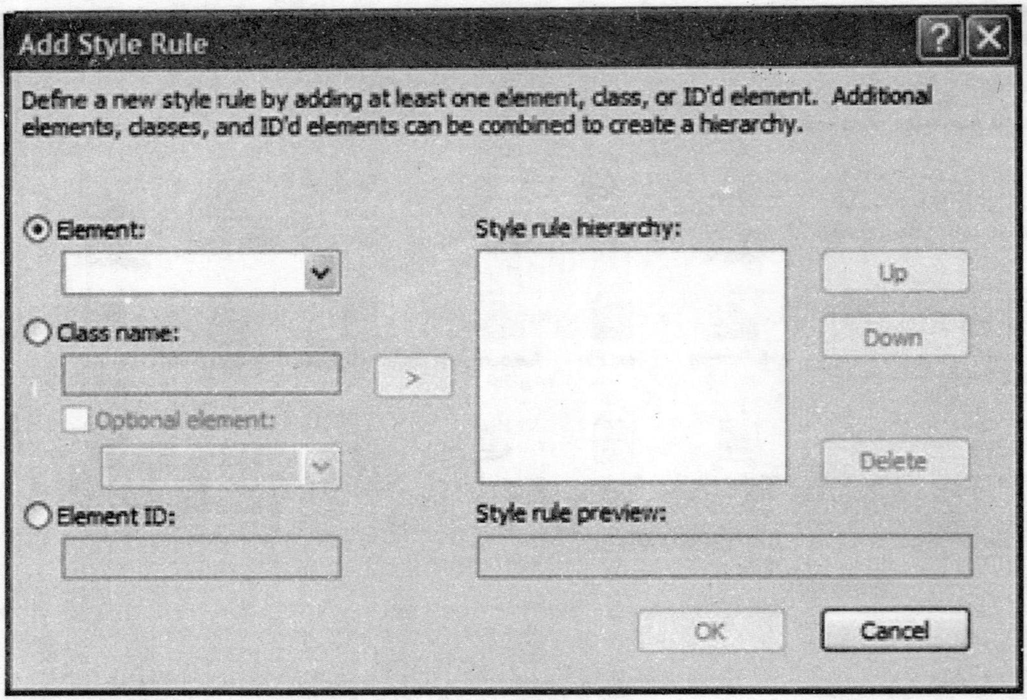

14. Now click on > button.
15. You may see the preview in Style rule preview:
16. Click OK.
17. Now your Style Sheet file code has been changed to following:

```
body {
}
P:first-letter  P:first-letter
{
}
```

Like this you can create the rules.

ADDING PROPERTIES TO STYLE SHEET RULES

Once the style rule has been created then you can add properties. For this perform the following steps:

1. In menu bar click Styles.
2. Now click Build Style...
3. Style Builder dialog box appears.

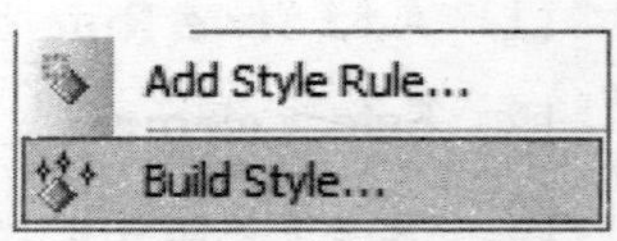

4. Under Font attributes, Select Color and then from drop-down list select White color.

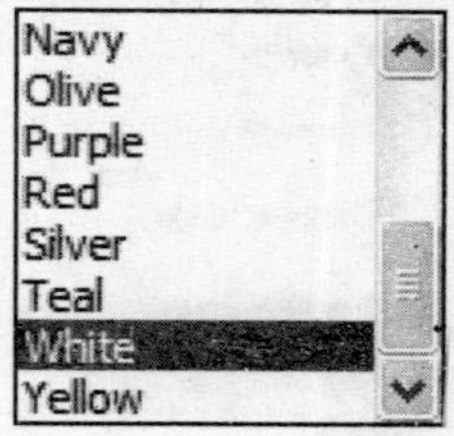

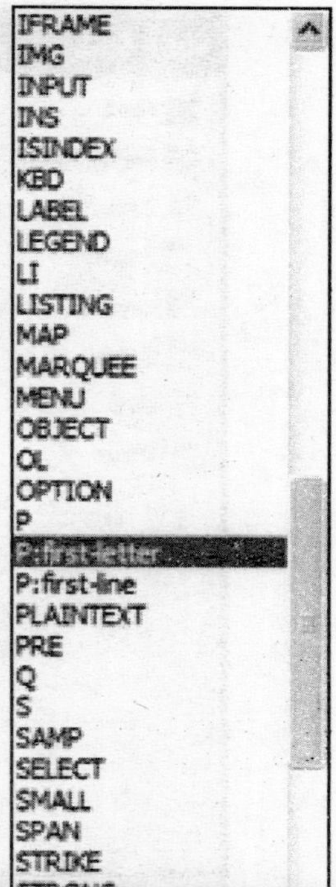

5. Now click OK Button.
6. At this stage your style sheet file has appended with following code:

```
body {
}
P:first-letter P:first-letter
{
  color: white;
}
```

Style sheet rule changes the appearance of other objects. Notice thing is they do not have their own appearance. These are abstract specifications and that's why style sheet does not have Design view.

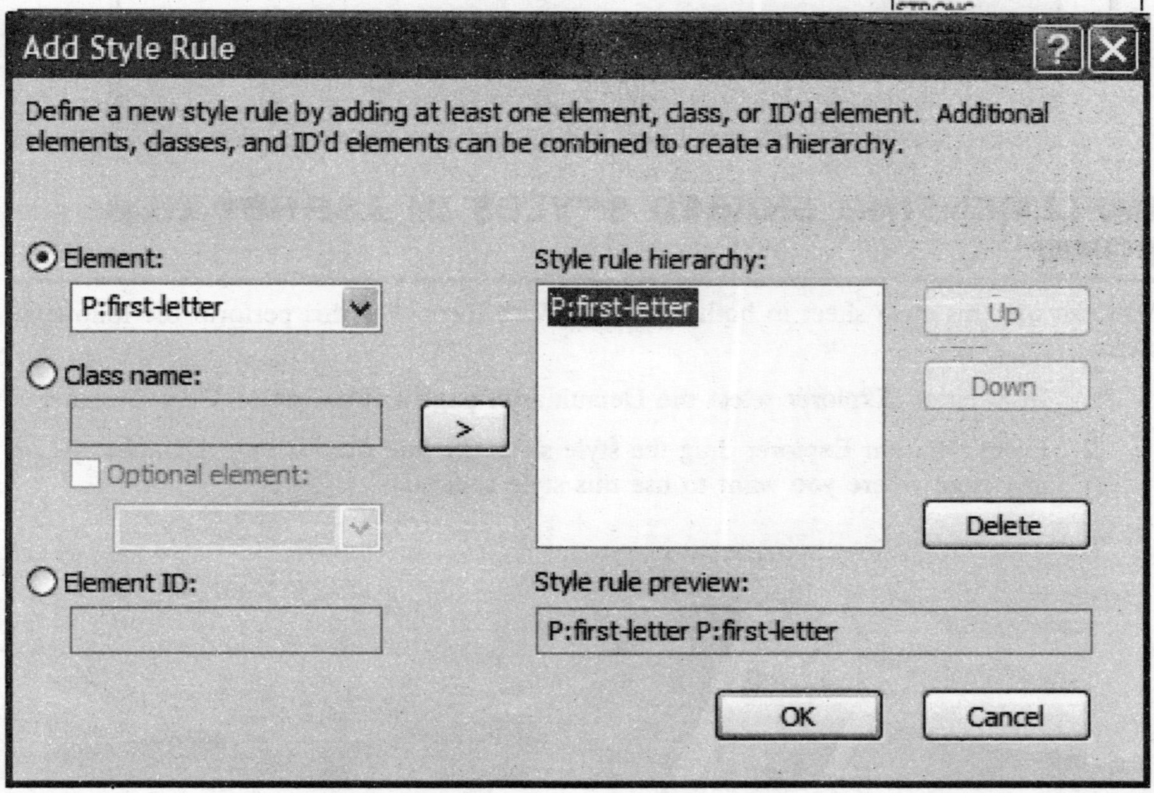

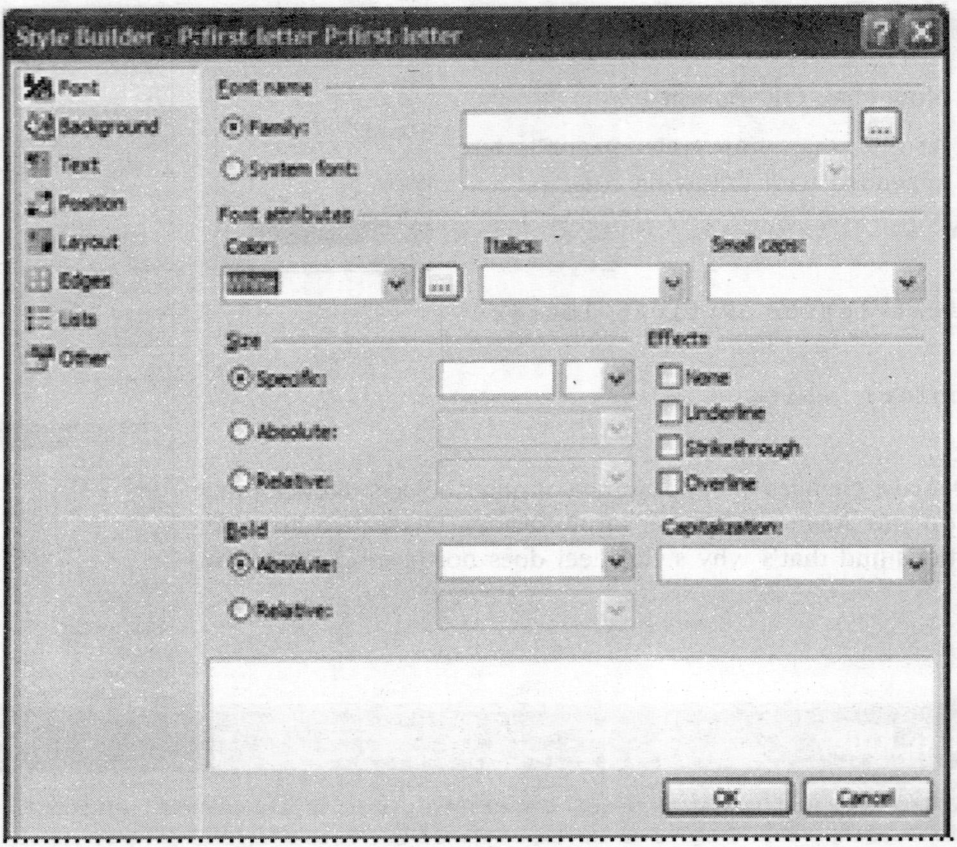

IMPLEMENTING SHARED STYLES IN ASP.NET WEB FORM

You can use this style sheet in both Master or Web form. For this perform the following steps:

1. In Solution Explorer select the Default.aspx page and switch to View Designer.
2. From Solution Explorer drag the style sheet file and drop it onto Default.aspx or any page where you want to use this style sheet file.

5 Questions

ANSWER THE FOLLOWING QUESTIONS

CHAPTER 1 — INTRODUCTION TO ASP USING HTML

1. What are Client side and Server side scripting?
2. Describe the following HTML tags with examples.

Start and End tags	Bold
Italic	Underline
Heading	Paragraph
Break	Font
Horizontal Line	Blockquote
Comments	Strikethrough
Big	Small
Subscript	Superscript
Link	Table
Form element	Text box
Check box	Radio Button
List box	Submit

3. Describe the following codes with examples.

HtmlAnchor Control	HtmlButton Control
HtmlForm Control	HtmlGeneric Control
HtmlImage Control	HtmlInputButton Control
HtmlInputCheckbox Control	HtmlInputFile Control
HtmlInputHidden Control	HtmlInputImage Control
HtmlInputRadioButton Control	HtmlInputText Control
HtmlSelect Control	HtmlTable Control

CHAPTER 2 — STANDARD CONTROLS OF ASP

1. Describe the following standard controls with examples.

AdRotator Control

BulletedList Control

Button Control

Calendar Control

Checkbox Control

Checkboxlist Control

DropDownList Control

FileUpload Control

HiddenField Control

HyperLink Control

Image Control

ImageButton Control

ImageMap control

Label Control

LinkButton Control

ListBox Control

Literal Control

MultiView Control

Panel Control

PlaceHolder Control

RadioButton Control

RadioButtonList Control

Substitution Control

Table Control

Textbox Control

Wizard Control

XML Control

2. Describe the following validation controls with examples.

RequiredFieldValidator Controls

RangeValidator Control

RegularExpressionValidator Control

CompareValidator Control

CustomValidator Control

ValidationSummary Control

CHAPTER 3 — OTHER CONTROLS OF ASP

1. Describe the following validation controls with examples.

RequiredFieldValidator Controls

RangeValidator Control

RegularExpressionValidator Control

CompareValidator Control

CustomValidator Control

ValidationSummary Control

2. Describe the following dailog box controls:

OpenFileDialog control | SaveFileDialog control

ColorDialog control | FontDialog control

FolderBrowserDialog control

3. Which are the user controls?

4. Describe how would you create, add and test the user controls?

CHAPTER 4 — MASTER PAGES AND CSS

1. How would you create a web site with master page

2. What are shared style sheets?

3. How would you add properties to the style sheet rules?

ISBN	TITLE	AUTHOR	PRICE	PAGES
CALL CENTERS				
8170082196	**Call Centers Made Easy**	Stephen Medcroft	Rs. 195.00	310
CISCO				
8170087481	**Enabling IP Routing with Cisco Routers**	R. Das, K. Chakrabarty	Rs. 295.00	486
817008749X	**Designing Networks with Cisco**	H. Pasricha, D. Jagu	Rs. 195.00	316
8170087503	**Cisco IP Routing Protocols: Troubleshooting Techniques**	V. Anand, K. Chakrabarty	Rs. 295.00	409
DATABASES				
8170089530	**DBMS—Complete Practical Approach**	Sharad Maheshwari, Ruchin Jain	Rs. 350.00	656
8170082404	**Learn to Program Visual Basic-Examples**	John Smiley	Rs. 295.00	482
8170082412	**Learn to Program Visual Basic-Databases**	John Smiley	Rs. 325.00	653
8170082420	**Learn to Program Visual Basic-Objects**	John Smiley	Rs. 325.00	670
817008475X	**IT Resources-Access 2002 VBA Programming Access**	Michele Amelot	Rs. 195.00	424
8170084512	**The Power of Oracle 9i**	Rajiv Parida, Vinod Sharma	Rs. 475.00	1035
8170088518	**Principles and Implementation of Data Warehousing**	Rajiv A. Parida	Rs. 295.00	487
817008864X	**DBA Study Guide OCP Prep Guide**	Nazar Abdul	Rs. 295.00	474
8170088658	**Oracle 11i—The Complete Reference**	Rashmi Anandi	Rs. 495.00	975
8131800067	**Toxonomy of Database Management System**	Aditya Kumar Gupta	Rs. 75.00	146
8131800385	**Introduction to SQL and PL/SQL**	Sharad Maheshwari, Ruchin Jain	Rs. 200.00	389
DOEACC 'O' LEVEL				
8170088089	**DOEACC 'O' Level Model Test Papers**	Ramesh Bangia	Rs. 175.00	296
8170089115	**DOEACC 'O' & 'A' Level Programming & Problem Solving Through 'C' Language (Model Test Paper with Solutions)**	Mukesh Sharma	Rs. 95.00	213
8170089069	**DOEACC 'O' & 'A' Level Business Systems (Model Test Paper with Solutions)**	Mukesh Sharma	Rs. 100.00	252
8170085640	**Programming and Problem Solving Through "C" Language**	Harsha Priya, R. Ranjeet	Rs. 95.00	306

ISBN	TITLE	AUTHOR	PRICE	PAGES
8170084474	**IT Tools and Applications**	Ramesh Bangia	Rs. 145.00	370
8170085594	**Business Systems**	Ramesh Bangia	Rs. 175.00	452
8170089514	**Internet & Web Design**	Ramesh Bangia	Rs. 150.00	300

ELECTRONIC COMMERCE

ISBN	TITLE	AUTHOR	PRICE	PAGES
8170085497	**Electronic Commerce**	Pete Loshin, John Vacca	Rs. 295.00	472
817008119X	**E-Commerce**	Mamta Bhusry	Rs. 95.00	215
8170083524	**Marketing in the Cyber Age**	Kurt Rohner	Rs. 295.00	223

HARDWARE/EMBEDDED SYSTEMS

ISBN	TITLE	AUTHOR	PRICE	PAGES
8170087473	**Essential Electronics for PC Technicians**	John W. Farber	Rs. 295.00	546
8170086264	**Grid Computing: A Practical Guide to Technology and Applications**	Ahmar Abbas	Rs. 295.00	408
8170088186	**CD Cracking Uncovered Protection Against Unsanctioned CD Copy**	Kris Kaspersky	Rs. 295.00	422
8170083435	**Practical Linux Programming: Device Drivers, Embedded Systems and the Internet**	Ashfaq A. Khan	Rs. 295.00	420
8170083575	**TCP/IP Application Layer Protocols for Embedded Systems**	M. Tim Jones	Rs. 295.00	460
8131800520	**PC Repair and Maintenance : A Practical Guide**	Joel Rosenthal, Kevin Irwin	Rs. 195.00	362
8131800768	**The A+ Certification and PC Repair Handbook**	Christopher A Crayton, Joel Z. Rosenthal	Rs. 495.00	888

INTERNET & WEB TECHNOLOGY

ISBN	TITLE	AUTHOR	PRICE	PAGES
8170083206	**The Internet Handbook for Writers, Students and Teachers**	Mary McGuire, Linda Stilborne	Rs. 195.00	276
8170084776	**Way in-Internet Getting Started**	Elizabeth Bramire	Rs. 95.00	165
8170088976	**Web Technology**	Ramesh Bangia	Rs. 250.00	560
8170087163	**Web Design with Macromedia Studio MX 2004**	Eric Hunley	Rs. 295.00	558
8170083400	**Professional Web Design (Techniques and Templates)**	Clint Eccher	Rs. 295.00	425
8170088046	**HTML, XHTML, CSS and XML**	Teodoru Gugoiu	Rs. 195.00	355
8170083583	**FrontPage 2000 for Visual Learners**	Chris Charuhas	Rs. 95.00	200
8170083591	**HTML & Java Script for Visual Learners**	Chris Charuhas	Rs. 95.00	200

ISBN	TITLE	AUTHOR	PRICE	PAGES
8170083605	**The Visual Learners Guide to Managing Web Projects**	Chris Charuhas	Rs. 95.00	130
8170083613	**Dreamweaver 4 for Visual Learners**	Chris Charuhas	Rs. 95.00	200
8170084768	**IT Resource-Implementing XML: Managing and Formatting Data**	Johhny Brochard	Rs. 125.00	279
8170089476	**Design Your Web World**	Sunil Jalota	Rs. 75.00	146

KEEPING AHEAD SERIES

ISBN	TITLE	AUTHOR	PRICE	PAGES
8170084652	**Keeping Ahead-Exchange 2000 Server**	Philippe Levesque	Rs. 145.00	285
8170084660	**Keeping Ahead-Windows 2000 Professional**	Jose Dardoigne	Rs. 175.00	388
8170084679	**Keeping Ahead-Windows 2000 Server**	Philippe Mathon	Rs. 175.00	360
8170084687	**Keeping Ahead-Linux Administration Kernel Version 2.0 to 2.2**	Bruno Guèrin	Rs. 125.00	240
8170084695	**Keeping Ahead-Using Linux Kernel Version 2.0 to 2.2**	Bruno Guèrin	Rs. 125.00	258
8170084709	**Keeping Ahead-Java 2**	Benjamin Aumaille	Rs. 145.00	284
8170084717	**Keeping Ahead-SQL Server 7**	Joelle Mosset	Rs. 145.00	329
8170084725	**Keeping Ahead-JavaScript and VBScript**	Benjamin Aumaille	Rs. 145.00	313
8170084733	**Keeping Ahead-C++ Programming Language**	Bruno Dubois	Rs. 125.00	234
8170084741	**Keeping Ahead-TCP/IP in the NT Environment**	Bruno Ferec	Rs. 125.00	230

MCSE

ISBN	TITLE	AUTHOR	PRICE	PAGES
817008489X	**MCSE-Administering SQL Server 7.0**	Jerome Gabillaud	Rs. 295.00	580
8170084903	**MCSE-Networking Essentials**	Jose Dordoigne	Rs. 245.00	453
8170084911	**MCSE-Windows 2000 Professional**	Jose Dordoigne	Rs. 325.00	665
817008492X	**MCSE-Windows 2000 Server**	Phillippe Mathon	Rs. 345.00	712

MULTIMEDIA AND ANIMATION

ISBN	TITLE	AUTHOR	PRICE	PAGES
8170088208	**3DS Max 6 Animation with Character Studio 4 and Plug-Ins**	Boris Kulagin, Dmitry Morozov	Rs. 175.00	216

Please write for a free color Firewall Media Catalog for details on the above books.

ISBN	TITLE	AUTHOR	PRICE	PAGES
8170088216	**Adobe Audition: Soundtracks for Digital Video**	Roman Petelin, Yury Petelin	Rs. 195.00	278
8170086205	**Building A Digital Human**	Ken Brilliant	Rs. 295.00	380
8170086213	**Making Digital Videos**	Ben Long	Rs. 295.00	284
8170087171	**Illustrating with Macromedia Flash ™ MX2004**	Robert Firbaugh	Rs. 245.00	366
8170082439	**Multimedia Basics-Technology (Vol. I)**	Andreas Holzinger	Rs. 195.00	312
8170082447	**Multimedia Basics-Learning (Vol. II)**	Andreas Holzinger	Rs. 195.00	326
8170082455	**Multimedia Basics-Design (Vol. III)**	Andreas Holzinger	Rs. 195.00	280
8170083532	**Maya Feature Creature Creations**	Todd Palamar	Rs. 295.00	376
8170083540	**Sound Forge Power**	Scott R. Garrigus	Rs. 195.00	344
8131800288	**Multimedia and Web Technology**	Ramesh Bangia	Rs. 395.00	878
813180044X	**Photoshop CS**	Shruti Lal	Rs. 195.00	434

NETWORKING

ISBN	TITLE	AUTHOR	PRICE	PAGES
817008721X	**Networking Essentials**	Jose Dordoigne	Rs. 195.00	453
8170089328	**TCP/IP Distributed System**	Vivek Acharya	Rs. 250.00	474
8170087023	**Computer Networks**	Ajit Kumar Singh	Rs. 95.00	181
8131800148	**The Real—world Network Troubleshooting Manual**	Alan Sugano	Rs. 295.00	396
817008203X	**Telecom & Networking Glossary**	Robert Mastin	Rs. 300.00	250
8170082048	**Data Networking Made Easy**	Karen Patten	Rs. 360.00	350
8170082056	**Digital Convergence**	Andy Covell	Rs. 300.00	234

OFFICE AUTOMATION

ISBN	TITLE	AUTHOR	PRICE	PAGES
8170089891	**Desk Top Publishing**	Dinesh Maidasani	Rs. 150.00	311
8170087805	**Learning Computer Fundamentals, MS Office and Internet & Web Technology**	Dinesh Maidasani	Rs. 95.00	301
8170087686	**MS-Word 2000 Thumb-Rules and Details**	Snigdha Banerjee	Rs. 175.00	390
8170089239	**Computer Accounting with Tally 7.2**	Firewall Media	Rs. 195.00	330

ON YOUR SIDE SERIES

ISBN	TITLE	AUTHOR	PRICE	PAGES
8170084830	**On your Side-Powerpoint 2002**	Andrew Blackburn	Rs. 145.00	282
8170084849	**On your Side-Excel 2002**	Adrienne Tommy	Rs. 125.00	275

Please write for a free color Firewall Media Catalog for details on the above books.

ISBN	TITLE	AUTHOR	PRICE	PAGES
8170084857	**On your Side-Word 2002**	Adrienne Tommy	Rs. 125.00	289
8170084865	**On your Side-Access 2002**	Adrienne Tommy	Rs. 125.00	303
8170084873	**On your Side-Frontpage 2002**	Andrew Blackburn	Rs. 95.00	245
8170084881	**On your Side-Windows XP**	Adrienne Tommy	Rs. 125.00	310
	OPERATING SYSTEMS			
8170087236	**Linux—A Practical Approach**	B. Mohamed Ibrahim	Rs. 95.00	187
8170088623	**Red Hat Linux Study Guide**	Vijay Shekhar	Rs. 350.00	635
8170088631	**Red Hat Linux-The Complete Bible**	Vijay Shekhar	Rs. 545.00	1176
8170089581	**Unix and Shell Programming**	Archana Verma	Rs. 80.00	137
8170089131	**Operating System Concepts**	P.S. Gill	Rs. 95.00	181
8170083427	**The MS-Windows XP Professional Handbook**	Louis Columbus	Rs. 295.00	330
8170084784	**Way in-Windows XP Home Edition**	Andrew Blackburn	Rs. 95.00	183
8170086221	**Cyber Rookies—Operating System Fundamentals**	D. Irtegov	Rs. 295.00	498
	PROGRAMMING			
8170087791	**The Art of Programming Through Flowcharts & Algorithms**	Anil Bikas Chaudhuri	Rs. 95.00	160
8170086248	**Preventative Programming Techniques: Avoid and Correct Common Mistakes**	Brian Hawkins	Rs. 295.00	322
8170083443	**Learning Computer Programming : It's not about Languages**	Mary Farrell	Rs. 295.00	375
8170086256	**Object-Oriented Programming: From Problem Solving to Java**	José M. Garrido	Rs. 295.00	360
817008931X	**Object-Oriented Programming-Concept and Implementation**	A. Rajesh	Rs. 95.00	182
8170089107	**Java: J2SE-5 A Practical Approach**	B. Mohammad Ibrahim	Rs. 175.00	332
8170089409	**Advance Java**	Gajendra Gupta	Rs. 175.00	305
8170088038	**Assembly Language Programming for Intel Processors Family**	Vasile Lungu	Rs. 295.00	577
8170088178	**The Assembly Programming Master Book**	Vlad Pirogov	Rs. 395.00	726
813180075X	**Java Messaging**	Eric Bruno	Rs. 295.00	480

ISBN	TITLE	AUTHOR	PRICE	PAGES
	PROGRAMMING - C#, C, C++			
8170083702	**The Power of C#**	Rajiv Parida	Rs. 295.00	576
8170085632	**Mastering Graphics Programming in 'C'**	Sudhir Dawra	Rs. 145.00	286
8170088879	**Programming in C and Numerical Analysis**	J.B. Dixit	Rs. 350.00	355
8170087074	**Mastering C Programs**	J.B. Dixit	Rs. 195.00	434
8170081262	**Programming in C**	J.B. Dixit	Rs. 295.00	506
8170087619	**Unix and C Programming**	Ashok Arora, Shefali Bansal	Rs. 295.00	606
817008878X	**C Interview Questions and Answers**	J. Rajaram	Rs. 75.00	139
8170089034	**Pragmatic C**	R.K. Jangda	Rs. 150.00	258
8170086140	**Data Structure for 'C' Programming**	Ajay Kumar	Rs. 145.00	290
8170081270	**Programming in C++**	J.B. Dixit	Rs. 260.00	602
8170088194	**Hackish C++ Pranks & Tricks**	Michael Flenov	Rs. 245.00	326
8170082889	**Basics of C++ Programming**	Nishant Kundalia	Rs. 95.00	168
8170083648	**Mastering C++ Programs**	J.B. Dixit	Rs. 295.00	598
817008623X	**Cyber Rookies—C++ Programming Fundamentals**	Chuck Easttom	Rs. 295.00	417
8131800202	**Data Structure using C++**	N. Jayalakshmi	Rs. 65.00	126
8170089123	**C++ Made Easy**	T.D. Malhotra	Rs. 250.00	449
8131800393	**C++ & Introduction to C#**	T.D. Malhotra, Rajeev A. Parida, A. Rajesh	Rs. 200.00	440
8131800350	**OOPS with C++**	M. Jaya Prasad	Rs. 150.00	317
	SECURITY			
8170083419	**Computer Forensics : Computer Crime Scene Investigation**	John Vacca	Rs. 445.00	731
8131800156	**Computer Evidence (Collection and Preservation)**	Christopher L.T. Brown	Rs. 295.00	394
8170083494	**Firewall Architecture for the Enterprise**	Norbert Pohlmann, Tim Crothers	Rs. 295.00	480
8170086272	**Net Spies**	Andrew Gauntlett	Rs. 195.00	210
3826607546	**Firewall Systems**	Norbert Pohlmann	Rs. 1630.00	544
8131800504	**Homeland Security Techniques and Technologies**	Jesus Mena	Rs. 295.00	346

ISBN	TITLE	AUTHOR	PRICE	PAGES
	ENGINEERING AND TECHNOLOGY			
817008718X	**Human Aspects of Software Engineering**	James E. Tomayko, Orit Hazzan	Rs. 195.00	338
8131800032	**Management Information Systems**	Avdhesh Gupta, Anurag Malik	Rs. 195.00	400
8170087953	**Human Computer Interaction**	Rajendra Ranjan Kumar	Rs. 95.00	210
8170088097	**Structured System Analysis and Design**	Preeti Gupta	Rs. 125.00	192
817008802X	**Autocad 2005 for Engineers**	Ionel Simion	Rs. 175.00	271
8170088054	**Digital Signal Processing Fundamentals**	Ashfaq A. Khan	Rs. 295.00	391
8131800164	**Digital Communication System Using System VUE**	Dennis Silage	Rs. 295.00	365
8170089719	**Foundations of Computer Science**	Ashok Arora	Rs. 250.00	386
817008363X	**Practical Project Management**	Ivan Bayross	Rs. 195.00	342
8131800806	**Digital Signal Processing using MATLAB and Wavelets**	Michael Weeks	Rs. 350.00	452
8131800792	**Classical Electrodynamics**	Hans C. Dhanian	Rs. 395.00	620
8131800512	**The Software Vulnerability Guide**	Herbert H. Thompson, Scott G. Chase	Rs. 195.00	368
8131800776	**Robot Modelling and Kinematics**	Rachid Manseur	Rs. 295.00	380
8131800369	**System Software**	M. Joseph	Rs. 95.00	185
	STRAIGHT TO THE POINT SERIES			
8170084601	**STTP : Word 2002**	Corinne Hervo	Rs. 45.00	154
817008461X	**STTP : Excel 2002**	Corinne Hervo	Rs. 45.00	153
8170084628	**STTP : Dreamweaver 4**	Corinne Hervo	Rs. 45.00	135
8170084636	**STTP : Flash 5**	Corinne Hervo	Rs. 45.00	183
8170084644	**STTP : Photoshop 6**	Corinne Hervo	Rs. 45.00	152
817008881X	**STTP : MS Office 2000**	Dinesh Maidasani	Rs. 125.00	290
8170086100	**STTP : MS Office 2003**	Dinesh Maidasani	Rs. 145.00	288
8170087651	**STTP : MS Word 2003**	Firewall Media	Rs. 60.00	150
8170088011	**STTP : Photoshop CS**	Firewall Media	Rs. 60.00	150
8170088143	**STTP : MS Excel 2003**	Firewall Media	Rs. 60.00	150
8170088151	**STTP : CorelDraw 12**	Firewall Media	Rs. 60.00	150
8131800105	**STTP : 3ds MAX 7**	Dinesh Maidasani	Rs. 95.00	182
8131800083	**STTP : Auto CAD 2006**	Dinesh Maidasani	Rs. 95.00	190
8131800245	**STTP : CorelDraw X3**	Dinesh Maidasani	Rs. 75.00	188

ISBN	TITLE	AUTHOR	PRICE	PAGES
8131800253	**STTP : Dreamweaver 8**	Dinesh Maidasani	Rs. 75.00	148
8131800237	**STTP : Photoshop CS2**	Dinesh Maidasani	Rs. 75.00	172
8170088380	**STTP : Tally 7.2**	Firewall Media	Rs. 175.00	322
8131800091	**STTP : Flash 8**	Dinesh Maidasani	Rs. 95.00	180
8131800407	**STTP : My SQL 5.0**	Dinesh Maidasani	Rs. 85.00	166
8131800458	**STTP : Microsoft Power Point 2003**	Dinesh Maidasani	Rs. 75.00	142

STUDIO FACTORY

ISBN	TITLE	AUTHOR	PRICE	PAGES
8170084792	**Studio Factory—Photoshop 6**	Christophe Aubry	Rs. 175.00	364
8170084806	**Studio Factory—Flash 5**	Sami Ben Yahiya	Rs. 145.00	314
8170084814	**Studio Factory—Dreamweaver Ultradev 4**	Phillippe Chatellier	Rs. 95.00	240
8170084822	**Studio Factory—Dreamweaver 4**	Christophe Aubry	Rs. 175.00	373
8170087643	**Studio Factory—Dreamweaver MX**	Christophe Aubry	Rs. 195.00	407
8170087627	**Studio Factory—Flash MX**	Arnaud Blanche	Rs. 145.00	337
817008766X	**Studio Factory—Photoshop 7**	Cyril Guerin	Rs. 195.00	420

LAXMI PUBLICATIONS (P) LTD

113, Golden House, Daryaganj, New Delhi-110002

Phone : **011 - 43 53 25 00**

Fax : **011 - 43 53 25 28**

EMAIL : info@laxmipublications.com

Website : www.laxmipublications.com

BRANCHES

- 129/1, IIIrd Main Road, IX Cross, Chamrajpet, **Bangalore** (*Phone* : 080-26 61 15 61)
- 26, Damodaran Street, T. Nagar, **Chennai** (*Phone* : 044-24 34 47 26)
- 43/1394D, St. Benedict's Road, Ernakulam North, **Cochin** (*Phone* : 0484-239 70 04)
- Pan Bazar, Rani Bari, **Guwahati** (*Phones* : 0361-254 36 69, 251 38 81)
- 4-2-453, Ist Floor, Ramkote, **Hyderabad** (*Phone* : 040-24 75 02 47)
- Adda Tanda Chowk, N.D. 365, **Jalandhar City** (*Phone* : 0181-222 12 72)
- 106/A, Ist Floor, S.N. Banerjee Road, **Kolkata** (*Phones* : 033-22 27 37 73, 22 27 52 47)
- 18, Madan Mohan Malviya Marg, **Lucknow** (*Phone* : 0522-220 95 78)
- 142-C, Victor House, Ground Floor, N.M. Joshi Marg, Lower Parel (W), **Mumbai** (*Phones* : 022-24 91 54 15, 24 92 78 69)
- Radha Govind Street, Tharpagna, **Ranchi** (*Phone* : 0651-230 77 64)